Differentiating Assessment in Middle and High School Mathematics and Science

Sheryn Spencer Waterman

EYE ON EDUCATION
6 DEPOT WAY WEST, SUITE 106
LARCHMONT, NY 10538
(914) 833–0551
(914) 833–0761 fax
www.eyeoneducation.com

Library of Congress Cataloging-in-Publication Data

Waterman, Sheryn Spencer.
Differentiating assessment in middle and high school mathematics and science / Sheryn Spencer Waterman.
    p. cm.
    ISBN 978-1-59667-107-2
1. Mathematics—Study and teaching (Middle school) 2. Mathematics—Study and teaching (Secondary) 3. Science—Study and teaching (Middle school) 4 Science—Study and teaching (Secondary) 5. Mathematical readiness. 6. Individualized instruction. 7. Learning ability—Testing. I. Title.
    QA11.2.W375 2008
    510.71'2—dc22

                                        2008046880

10 9 8 7 6 5 4 3 2

Also Available from EYE ON EDUCATION

**Differentiating Assessment in
Middle and High School English and Social Studies**
Sheryn Spencer Waterman

**Handbook on Differentiated Instruction
for Middle and High Schools**
Sheryn Spencer Northey

Formative Assessment: Responding to Your Students
Harry Grover Tuttle

Differentiated Assessment for Middle and High School Classrooms
Deborah Blaz

**Teacher-Made Assessments:
Connecting Curriculum, Instruction, and Student Learning**
Christopher R. Gareis and Leslie W. Grant

**Short Cycle Assessment:
Improving Student Achievement Through Formative Assessment**
Susan Lang, Todd Stanley and Betsy Moore

**Formative Assessment for English Language Arts:
A Guide for Middle and High School Teachers**
Amy Benjamin

**Performance-Based Learning and Assessment
in Middle School Science**
K. Michael Hibbard

**Assessment in Middle and High School Mathematics:
A Teacher's Guide**
Daniel Brahier

**A Collection of Performance Tasks and Rubrics:
Primary School Mathematics**
Charlotte Danielson and Pia Hansen Powell

Upper Elementary School Mathematics
Charlotte Danielson

Middle School Mathematics
Charlotte Danielson

High School Mathematics
Charlotte Danielson and Elizabeth Marquez

Meet the Author

Sheryn Spencer Waterman is an educational consultant and coach who specializes in curriculum design, differentiation, assessment, and literacy. Her many accomplishments include "Teacher of the Year" in two schools, National Board Certification (renewed in 2007), Founding Fellow for the Teacher's Network Leadership Institute, and founding interim President of the North Carolina Association of Literacy Coaches. She came to the field of education after a career as a psychotherapist and consultant. She has worked on many local, state, regional, and national projects to promote quality teaching. She is also a doctoral student at the University of North Carolina at Greensboro.

When she was known as Sheryn Spencer Northey, she wrote the highly successful *Handbook on Differentiated Instruction for Middle and High Schools.*

Free Downloads

Many of the examples discussed and displayed in this book are can be downloaded and printed out by anyone who has purchased this book. Book buyers have permission to download and print out these Adobe Acrobat documents.

You can access these downloads by visiting Eye On Education's Web site: www.eyeoneducation.com. Click on FREE Downloads. Or search or browse our Web site from our homepage to find this book and then scroll down for downloading instructions.

You'll need your book-buyer access code: **WAM-7107-2**

Index of Downloads

Table of Contents

1

Differentiated Assessment

Introduction

Assessment is probably the most important aspect of the learning experience. In fact, I suggest generally that the ratio of instruction to assessment should be approximately 1 to 4. For example, for every 10 minutes of instruction, the teacher should consider including approximately 40 minutes of assessment. More than allowing teachers and students to know what students already know and what they are learning or have learned, assessment supports instruction so that learning can take place.

In addition to being critically important to instruction, assessments that address students' needs are the most useful. Focusing on how teachers might differentiate assessment should greatly improve learning outcomes. This book provides an overview of assessment in conjunction with differentiation, an explanation of general differentiated assessment strategies, three chapters of examples differentiated by readiness for at-risk, average, and gifted or highly advanced students, and a chapter that shows how to put several assessment strategies together in a differentiated unit of study.

Some Concepts to Understand

There are many important issues to consider as we explore differentiated assessment. First, we should define the important terms that help us understand how learning, assessment, and evaluation interact. Figure 1.1 is an interesting visual adapted from Trussell-Cullen (1998, p. 7).

Figure 1.1. Learning→Assessment→Evaluation Loop→Learning, etc.

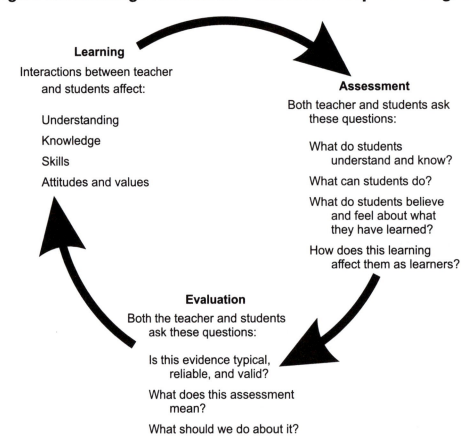

Defining Differentiated Assessment

Keeping these distinctions in mind, this book will focus on the "assessment" part of these concepts. We define "differentiation" as adjustments teachers make to address the learning needs of all students. (Northey, 2005; Tomlinson, 1995, 1999, 2003; Wormeli, 2006) When we combine assessment with differentiation, we can say that "differentiated assessment" is the process of finding out in a fair way what each individual student knows, understands, and can do (KUD), how they feel about what they have learned, and how they feel about themselves as learners.

Here is a list of criteria for good assessments suggested by Rick Wormeli (2006, pp. 39–41; see his book for a full discussion of each one).

Good assessment

- ◆ Increases learning rather than merely documenting it
- ◆ Chooses what is most important for students to learn
- ◆ Helps inform instruction
- ◆ Goes on throughout the unit of study and never saved for only "the end"

♦ Addresses knowledge, understanding, and skill development in a meaningful way

♦ Is authentic either to a real-world experience or to the way the information was taught

♦ Shows clear and valid information about what students have actually learned

♦ Is reliable across time and across classes of students

♦ Is timed well to check for learning

♦ Is integrated with other subjects

♦ Requires use of a variety of tools

♦ Helps teachers determine students' misunderstanding of the what students are learning

♦ Asks for students' input

♦ Is varied and differentiated

If teachers want to become skilled at implementing differentiated assessment in their classrooms, they might address these six parts of assessment planning as follows in Figure 1.2.

Figure 1.2. Six Parts of Planning Differentiated Assessment

1. **Students' needs:**	Who are the students in terms of: (a) readiness, (b) interests, and (c) learning and thinking styles, and what do they already know about the topic?
2. **Curriculum:**	What enduring essential knowledge (EEK) (expressed as essential questions [EQ]) do these students need to know, understand, and do (KUD)? Note that the measurable objective(s) is listed separately in Part 3 below but is also included in the curriculum.
3. **Measurable objectives:**	How will the teacher measure that learning?
4. **Differentiation:**	How should the teacher differentiate the assessment to meet students' learning needs?
5. **Procedures:**	What procedures will the teacher follow to implement the assessment?
6. **Assessment audit:**	How will teachers evaluate the alignment of the assessment(s) and procedures so that they have a clear picture of what each student knows, understands, and can do related to the content?

Students' Needs

In the first step of this implementation process, the teacher should assess students' readiness, interests, and learning or thinking styles. The following sections are an overview of how we should think about these factors.

Readiness

Assessment and the Zone of Proximal Development

When teachers plan assessments for students, they need to make certain to align them with students' readiness to learn. If the assessment is too simple or not sensitive to the students' level of development, then students may feel less motivated to stretch toward higher levels of learning. Teachers should be aware of what Vygotsky (1978) calls the "zone of proximal development" (ZPD), which is defined as the difference between what a person can do alone and what the person needs help to do. Most teachers know early in the year how well their students read, how well they solve learning problems, and how motivated they are to learn. If the teacher needs specific tools to assess these issues, Northey (2005) has several ideas for assessing reading, interests, and learning styles. Teachers must also at times use materials above or below the readiness level of some or all of their students. Picture books on the lower end and computer-generated explanations on the upper end can be excellent resources for differentiating content, but teachers need to make sure students do not feel demeaned or frustrated by these resources. Teachers also need to make sure to constantly inspire students to learn at higher and higher levels. Assessments that pay attention to the ZPD stretch students toward greater depth of knowledge and independence as learners. Teachers need to make sure to challenge students toward their highest capacity without overwhelming them. This balance within the ZPD is the key to successful differentiated assessment.

Interests

Teachers should take time to learn students' interests and emotional investment in their subject area (e.g., math, English) as well as individual units of study (e.g., decimals, plot of a story). As we know, motivation plays an important role in students' achievement. The teacher may use interests on certain areas to leverage student engagement in less interesting, but necessary, topics of learning. For example, a teacher who knows her students are interested in basketball can use basketball themes to teach difficult math or English concepts.

Learning and Thinking Styles

Teachers should find and administer surveys to determine students' learning styles. It is important that teachers keep in mind that learning and thinking styles are not static and that they can change based on the topic. Figure 1.3 is a short chart of some of the most popular learning and thinking styles.

Figure 1.3. Popular Learning and Thinking Styles

Number grouped by	Name of Inventory and Where to Find It
Three	1. Kinesthetic, Visual, or Auditory—Learning Channels: Preference checklist from Lynn O'Brien, (1990) 2. Creative, Analytical, or Practical—Thinking Styles from Richard Sternberg (1997)
Four	1. Imaginative, Investigative, Realistic, or Analytical— What Kind of Fruit are You? from Kathleen Butler (1987) 2. Mastery, Interpersonal, Understanding, and Self-Expressive—Silver, Strong, and Perini (2007) 3. Visual, Auditory, Kinesthetic, and Tactual—Rita and Kenneth Dunn (1993)
Five or more	1. Narrative, Logical, Foundational, Aesthetic, or Experiential—Entry Points for learning Howard Gardner (1993) 2. Verbal/Linguistic, Logical/Mathematical, Spatial, Bodily Kinesthetic, Musical, Interpersonal, Intrapersonal, Naturalist—the Multiple Intelligences Checklist—Howard Gardner (1993)
See http://eliot.needham.k12.ma.us/technology/di2/styles.htm for an exceptional overview of learning styles.	

At the beginning of Chapters 3, 4, and 5, teachers will find a detailed explanation of students' readiness levels as follows: at risk, average, and gifted or highly advanced. Chapter 3 is leveled for at-risk students; Chapter 4 is leveled for average students; and Chapter 5 is leveled for gifted or highly advanced students. Within each chapter teachers will find a description of special factors and issues related to readiness grouping. Each strategy also addresses students' interests and learning and thinking styles.

Curriculum

If teachers plan to differentiate assessment, they must have a working understanding of the major aspects of curriculum planning. It is critical that teachers determine meaningful curriculum goals that address students' needs in the context of mandated curriculum standards. If teachers do not use some method of clearly determining the direction for learning, they will not be able to assess effectively. When most teachers sign their teaching contracts, they agree to teach some form of determined curriculum, such as a standard course of study (SCOS). All assessment plans should flow from this. Figure 1.4 offers a brief explanation of some helpful concepts for teachers to plan useful assessment goals.

Figure 1.4. Parts of Curriculum

Title	Abbreviation	Explanation
Standard course of study	SCOS	Most states have curriculum standards that teachers are required to address. These standards may have goals and objectives that teachers can easily incorporate into their unit plans. Often they need to be "unpacked" or analyzed (pulled apart) so that the teacher can determine how to translate these standards for student learning.
Essential enduring knowledge (also know as: big idea, enduring understanding, etc.; here we call it "understanding.")	EEK	The EEK represents the core of the unit of study. It is what teachers want their students to remember from a unit of study for the rest of their lives (enduring). Having a well-conceptualized EEK is critical to planning differentiated assessments. When teachers are dealing with students who may need more time to learn, the EEK can help that teacher concentrate on ideas that have high priority so that no one will waste critical learning time on less important aspects of the topic or concept.
Essential questions	EQs	Essential questions make the unit topic relevant through the inquiry that is embedded in the notion of learning. Students might ask these questions with teacher help, or the teacher might pose them with student approval. Skills, knowledge, understanding, and objectives must answer these questions.
Knowledge, understanding, and can do	KUDs	In unit planning, this is a thorough and accurate list of the things students will know, understand, and be able to do as a result of the learning activities. Differentiated assessment is impossible to design without a clear idea of all the things students need to know, understand, and do.
Measurable objectives	MOs	The teachers' objectives must be measurable and must answer the EQs. To write a measurable objective, teachers must think about moving up a taxonomy of thinking skills for the thinking verb part of the objective (e.g., students will generate, create, apply, etc.). They should also write the product, response criterion or criteria, and content to write a comprehensive measurable objective.

In Chapters 3 through 5, as a way of introducing each assessment strategy, teachers will note a chart that provides an overview of curriculum goals. An example of the standard course of study is omitted because each district or state will have its own language. The chart looks like Figure 1.5.

Figure 1.5. Curriculum

SCOS	Essential Question (EQ)	Know	Understand	Do

Note: For the purpose of clarity, the EEK is incorporated within the EQs and KUDs and Curriculum Goals is shortened to Curriculum. *Also, the Measurable Objective(s) (MOs), although addressed separately, should be part of the Curriculum.*

Measurable Objectives

In Figure 1.2, part 3 of major differentiated assessment strategies includes a suggested measurable objective or objectives. This objective includes the following parts:

♦ An introductory phrase: "Students will or students will be able to…"

♦ A defining thinking verb from "New Bloom," for example, thinking verbs range in thinking skills from "recalling" to "producing"

♦ A product, for example, ranging in complexity from "a list" to "an invention"

♦ A statement about a specific quantitative or qualitative criterion for a sufficient response (Teachers can note responses that go above and beyond the standards they set at the beginning of the unit.)

♦ Specified content the teacher will assess

The generic template is shown in Figure 1.6.

Figure 1.6. Measurable Objective Template

Introduction	Thinking Verb	Product	Response Criterion	Content
For example: Students will…	recall	in order to list	at least five important facts	that define plant and animal cells.

Differentiation

When teachers know the students' needs in Figure 1.2, part 1, they will be able to address those needs in terms of a differentiation plan.

Teachers will see this chart as follows (Figure 1.7).

Figure 1.7. Differentiation Plan

Readiness—	Interests—	Learning styles—
students' or the classes' level of ability or capacity to be successful independently or with help on any given learning task	students' or the classes' naturally found interests that inspire them to learn any given task	students' best or favorite mode of learning on any given task (Noting that the preferred style may shift given the task)

Procedures

For each major differentiation assessment strategy, teachers will see a detailed list of steps they might take to implement it. They will also find specific and general examples to help them duplicate the idea or adapt it to meet their specific needs.

Assessment Audit

Each teacher needs to conduct an audit of the assessment strategy with his or her own students. Figure 1.8 is a useful template to check for assessment alignment. Figure 1.9 shows the Differentiating Assessment: Six-Part Template.

Figure 1.8. Differentiated Assessment Audit*

1.	How did the assessment of students' needs match the assessment strategy or strategies for the unit of study? Was anyone left out? Why? How?
2.	How did assessment strategy or strategies match the curriculum goals for the unit of study?
3.	How were the needs of every child represented in each differentiated assessment strategy or strategies?
4.	How did the measurable objective show best evidence of student achievement for the lesson or unit of study?
5.	How did the assessment strategy or strategies match content?
6.	How did this assessment strategy or strategies work overall:

$$1 \qquad 2 \qquad 3 \qquad 4 \qquad 5$$

(Circle 1 = low and 5 = high)

*Teachers can conduct an audit for each strategy or for the strategies they used to assess a unit of study.

Figure 1.9. Differentiating Assessment: Six-Part Template

1. Students' Needs (described in detail)				
2. Curriculum				
SCOS	Essential Question (EQ)	Know	Understand	Do (See MO below)
3. Measurable Objectives				
The generic template is as follows				
Introduction	Thinking Verb(s)	Product	Response Criterion	Content
4. Differentiation				
Readiness		Interests		Learning Styles
5. Assessment Procedures—Listed by steps				
6. Assessment Audit (see above)				

Concepts Critical to Effective Differentiated Assessments

Focus on Competence—Revision Mentality

Assessment strategies will differ based on the philosophical approach a teacher takes toward teaching and learning; however, regardless of what the teacher believes, it is important that the focus of instruction is on students gaining competence rather than teachers covering material so that they can issue a grade. With any perspective, the bottom line needs to be that the work is not finished until it is the best a student can do. For formative assessments, it is critical that teachers allow students to learn from their mistakes and to revise if what they have produced is substandard. The student might be the judge of when the work is finished rather than the teacher. From this perspective the revision process becomes an important and necessary step in the learning process. If a student completes a task perfectly every time, then the teacher may wonder if the assessment is truly challenging. Instead of giving a student an "F" as feedback on his or her work, the teacher might give the feedback as "Not yet." These two words are far more encouraging than an "F" for "Failure."

Assessment and Motivation

The best method of motivating learning is using assessment to help students feel they are successfully learning. Brain-based and cognitive researchers have been promoting the idea for some time now that the brain seeks complexity and wants to learn. Some teachers fail to realize the motivational impact of assessment in motivation. They might spend inordinate time and energy designing elaborate reward systems when they could get even more student motivation from cleverly designed assessments.

Time, the Learning Gap, and a Viable Curriculum

It is important that teachers make sure they have enough time to assess the most important knowledge and concepts for all students because the gap between those who are educated and those who struggle gets ever wider if instructional practices do not address the needs of all students. Also according to research (Marzano, 2003) many state-mandated curricula are not viable in allowing adequate time for all students to demonstrate mastery of their goals and objectives; therefore, teachers must prioritize those that might be most meaningful for their students' survival and well-being in their communities. If teachers take the time all students need for mastery rather than letting pacing guides rush them into coverage, they may actually save the time they might need for reteaching. Wiggins' & McTighe's (1998) "Three Circle Audit" is a great tool to help teachers determine their priorities. The critical idea to keep in mind is "What do you think your students should remember about this topic for the rest of their lives?" That is what you focus your assessment efforts on.

Differentiating Assessment in the Twenty-First Century

Differentiated assessment is important as we ask our students to develop twenty-first century skills. Students need to learn facts that are critical to their content area, but they need to learn them in the context of solving academic or real-world problems. Too many teachers plan assessments that determine if students have recalled facts related to their content areas, and they seem to be convinced that students must continue to recall facts, or they will not pass the test or be prepared for the next grade level. Most assessments of learning have moved beyond this low level of thinking. Teachers need to understand that they are short-changing their students by taking too much of the precious learning time to find out if students remember these facts isolated from problem solving. They need to *prioritize* teaching students how to learn facts as they analyze, apply, create, and evaluate them to solve problems.

We must adjust our thinking about standard forms of assessment, such as multiple choice tests or short answer tests of factual knowledge. By doing this we make room and time for a new level of competence. Within the information age, we realize that students no longer need to learn a set of facts that will help them succeed in a simple society. Our society is now highly complex and global. Teachers need to begin designing assessments that address the demands of the twenty-first century. As we look at differentiated assessment, we need to keep in mind that we need to assess students' abilities (Figure 1.10).

Figure 1.10. Twenty-First Century Skills

Digital Age Literacy	**Basic, Scientific, and Technological Literacy** ♦ Read critically ♦ Write persuasively ♦ Think logically ♦ Solve complex problems in science and mathematics **Visual and Information Literacy** ♦ Use visualization skills to decipher, interpret, note patterns, and communicate using imagery ♦ Assess information efficiently and effectively ♦ Evaluate information critically and completely ♦ Use information accurately and creatively **Cultural Literacy and Global Awareness** ♦ Know, understand, and appreciate other cultures ♦ Know, understand, and appreciate virtual realities.
Inventive Thinking and Intellectual Capital	**Adaptability, Managing Complexity, and Self-Direction** ♦ React independently to changing conditions ♦ Self-direct learning ♦ Analyze new conditions as they arise ♦ Identify new skills to deal with new conditions ♦ Independently make a plan to respond to new conditions ♦ Take contingencies into account ♦ Anticipate changes ♦ Understand how systems are interconnected. **Curiosity, Creativity, and Risk Taking** ♦ Adjust and adapt to changing situations ♦ Exercise curiosity and creativity **Higher-Order Thinking and Sound Reasoning** ♦ Plan, design, execute, and evaluate problems using technological tools

Interactive Communication— Social and Personal Skills	**Teaming and Collaboration** ♦ Work in teams to accomplish complex tasks ♦ Use technology to provide virtual workplaces for more timely and repetitive collaborations **Personal and Social Responsibility** ♦ Accept responsibility for ethical value judgments that guide the application of science and technology in society **Interactive Communication** ♦ Understand how to use technological communications ♦ Know the etiquette of various technological environments
Quality, State of the Arts, Results	**Prioritizing, Planning, and Managing Results** ♦ Demonstrate flexibility and creativity to anticipate unexpected outcomes of planning, managing, and anticipating contingencies related to project goal setting **Effective Use of Real World Tools** ♦ Use digital tools to help people solve problems for themselves ♦ Choosing the appropriate tools for a task and applying them to real world situations to promote creativity, construction of models, preparation of publications, and other creative works ♦ Focus on "know how" and "know who" rather than just "know what" as most important information **High-Quality Results with Real-World Application** ♦ Build authentic products with a variety of tools ♦ Develop deep insights concerning whatever tools are used

"Twenty-First Century Skills," retrieved November 25, 2007 at http://www.ncrel.org/sdrs/.

As we design differentiated assessments, we need to keep these twenty-first century skills in mind. We also need to constantly remind ourselves that the purpose of anything we teach our students results in their growth toward academic, social, and emotional competence. Here are some core skills teachers should remember to make sure they are including in differentiated assessments of students' work.

♦ *Reading* not just for understanding but for evaluating

♦ *Writing* to persuade

♦ *Thinking* logically at high levels to solve problems in our complex world

♦ *Using technology* to access information and to solve problems

What Is Developmentally Appropriate in Zeros and Make-Up Work?

When teachers think of assessing students to help prepare them for college and/or the world of work in the twenty-first century, they need to remember that students may only care about the present. Most students cannot conceive of themselves as potential adults in the real world or care about how their lives will be more than two or three years from the present. As teachers assess students, they need to be sensitive to their students' levels of development and make their assessments relevant to them. As teachers think about grading students and holding them accountable, they need to keep in mind that it may be more important to get the students to do the work rather than to give them a zero and tell them that they cannot make it up. Some teachers are concerned that they should not accept late work because they need to teach their students a lesson about meeting deadlines and being responsible. Teachers need to keep in mind two things. First, their students are still young and not developmentally sophisticated enough for the same standards as adults. Second, there are many examples in the real world that tell us just because you fail to meet a deadline, you still have to do what is expected. For example, just because you might be late paying a bill, you still have to pay it. As a matter or fact, you usually have to pay even more. Teachers should avoid giving zeroes, but they should also make sure students do the assigned work. Most often parents or administrators will help the teacher insist that students complete the work. For more discussion of this important aspect of differentiated assessment, see Wormeli (2006). If teachers cannot find a way to get students to do the work, they could at least use a point system that counteracts the devastating effects of putting a zero in the average.

Looking at Assessment Examples through the Lens of the Cognitive Process Dimension by Anderson and Colleagues

The work of Anderson, et al. (2001), also known as "New Bloom" informs the measurable objectives segment of the assessment explanation. When Anderson and colleagues revised Bloom's Taxonomy, they devised a method of categorizing cognitive processes that seems highly relevant to planning differentiated assessment. See their book for a full discussion of their ideas; however, here is a quick summary of their 6 main categories and 19 subcategories and how a teacher might address them through differentiated assessment. In Figure 1.11, I have summarized their definitions of cognitive processes and included how the teacher might differentiate the assessment of these processes.

Figure 1.11. Updated Bloom by Anderson, et al. (2001)

1. **Remember**—Retrieving information from the long-term memory		
1.1 Recognition	Defined as: Matching presented information with knowledge located in long-term memory. Also known as *identifying*.	Differentiating assessment: True/False, forced choice (multiple choice is the most popular), and matching are the three types. To differentiate these kinds of assessments the teacher might use games and tournaments to make them more engaging for all types of learners.
1.2 Recalling	Defined as: Getting relevant information from long-term memory. Also known as *retrieving*.	Differentiating assessment: To make this type of cognition most relevant to various learners, the teacher may embed the recall task in a larger high-interest problem.
2. **Understand**—Constructing meaning from instruction *Important:* If the teacher is to assess any higher-level cognitive function, the material presented must be new so that the student cannot rely on memory instead of higher-level thinking.		
2.1 Interpreting	Defined as: Changing from one type of representation to another. Also known as *clarifying, paraphrasing*.	Differentiating assessment: Assessment formats in which the teacher presents information in one form and students either construct or select the same information in a different form. Having students construct the information will elevate the assessment for advanced students. Struggling learners may feel more successful if the teacher allows them to select the answer.
2.2 Exemplifying	Defined as: Finding examples of a concept or principle. Also known as *illustrating*.	Differentiating assessment: This category provides an opportunity for the teacher to infuse artistic methods of constructing an answer to demonstrate cognitive mastery.
2.3 Classifying	Defined as: Deciding if something belongs to a category. Also known as: *categorizing, subsuming*.	Differentiating assessment: To assess learning students must either select a response or participate in a sorting task. Using a sorting task to place items in multiple categories can make this category a high-level learning experience for advanced students. Selecting a response makes it easier for struggling students.

2.4 Summarizing	Defined as: Determining a general theme or major points. Also known as *generalizing*.	Differentiating assessment: Teachers can make this category a high-level assessment experience for advanced students by asking them to construct information that is theme-based conceptualization rather than a summary of facts or events. Teachers can make it easier for struggling students by teaching them step by step methods of summarizing using graphic organizers and direct instruction.
2.5 Inferring	Defined as: Drawing logical conclusions from presented information. Also known as *predicting*.	Differentiating assessment: Common assessments for this cognitive category are completion tasks, analogy tasks, and oddity tasks. One way to make these assessments higher level for advanced students is to ask them to explain their underlying thinking for choosing their answer. One way to scaffold these tasks for struggling students is to provide lists of possible answers to complete the sentence or analogy.
2.6 Comparing	Defined as: Determining correspondence between ideas. Also known as *contrasting, matching*.	Differentiating assessment: Using cognitive-mapping strategies with some of the map filled in can provide scaffolding for struggling learners. Asking students to determine a full list of criteria on which to base comparing and contrasting can make this process higher level for advanced students.
2.7 Explaining	Defined as: Noting the cause and effect of something. Also known as constructing models.	Differentiating assessment: There are several possible assessment tasks for this cognitive category: reasoning, troubleshooting, redesigning, and predicting. All of these tasks can be designed to challenge the advanced learner because the problem through which they need to reason, or troubleshoot, redesign, or predict based on a change can be high level. The teacher may provide struggling students with scaffolding, such as helpful examples and partial completion of steps.

3. **Apply**—Using information or procedure in a situation		
3.1 Executing	Defined as: Using a procedure to perform a familiar task. Also known as *carrying out*.	Differentiating assessment: In this cognitive category teachers may differentiate the assessment based on the complexity and detail involved in addressing a specific task. Teachers might also provide graphic organizers to scaffold the task solution process for struggling learners.
3.2 Implementing	Defined as: Using a procedure to perform an unfamiliar task. Also known as *using*.	Differentiating assessment: The teacher may level these assessment tasks according to their difficulty. Teachers may also provide scaffolding organizers to help struggling students with procedures.
4. **Analyze**—Breaking something into parts to determine the purpose of the parts in relation to the overall purpose of the whole		
4.1 Differentiating	Defined as: Distinguishing between relevant and irrelevant parts of presented material. Also known as *discriminating*.	Differentiating assessment: Teachers may use a *constructed response* in which they give the students materials from which to choose to solve the task, and the students must decide which materials they need; or *selection task,* which asks students to determine which parts of the information provided about the task are relevant. The teacher can differentiate this assessment based on the "fuzziness" of the problems the students must solve. For advanced students the task may be complex, and for struggling students the task might be less fuzzy and require more guidance from the teacher in the way of organizers and other teacher input.
4.2 Organizing	Defined as: Deciding how elements fit or function within a structure or imposing a structure on material. Also known as *structuring*.	Differentiating assessment: To differentiate this cognitive category the teacher might use differing levels of material to ask students to outline. Or the teacher might make a selection task more challenging by asking students to select the best hierarchies from which to organize the leveled materials.

4.3 Attributing	Defined as: Determining what might be underlying presented material (e.g., author's purpose). Also known as *deconstructing.*	Differentiating assessment: Teachers may differentiate the assessment of this cognitive category based on the material from which they ask the students to construct or select a response. Also constructing a response from a prompt such as "Explain the author's purpose for writing this poem" can be more challenging than selecting that purpose from a list of purposes. It might also be easier to select from a different type of selection process in which the student decides if the author would agree or disagree with a specific statement the teacher makes about the material.
5. Evaluate—Making a judgment based on criteria		
5.1 Checking	Defined as: Determining the following: inconsistencies, effectiveness, consistency within a process or product. Also known as *testing.*	Differentiating assessment: The teacher may differentiate this cognitive assessment category by asking struggling students to check operations or products the teacher supplies. The teacher might also allow them to complete this kind of assignment in a small group with stronger students or with a stronger partner. The teacher might also give possible selection ideas. Teachers can make this process higher level by asking advanced students to check the accuracy and quality of products or processes they have created themselves.
5.2 Critiquing	Defined as: Determining the inconsistencies and appropriateness of a product or process based on external criteria. Also known as *judging.*	Differentiating assessment: To make this type of assessment easier, the teacher might provide the list of simple (positive and negative) criteria on which the students must judge a teacher-determined process or product. To make it harder the teacher might ask students to judge their own hypotheses or creations based on complex criteria they determine.

6. **Create**—Inserting new or reorganizing old elements to form a functional whole		
6.1 Generating	Defined as: Coming up with another idea based on criteria. Also known as *hypothesizing.*	Differentiating assessment: The teacher may differentiate these two subtypes of assessments for this cognitive category: *consequences tasks* (in which students list all the possible consequences of a specified event) and *uses tasks* (in which the student lists all the possible uses for an object). The teacher might differentiate this assessment by using events and objects that are highly relevant, well-known, and interesting to at-risk students. For example, the teacher might use a pop culture or sports event or object from which students must generate their lists. The teacher can make this assessment more challenging by making it more abstract and fuzzy for advanced learners.
6.2 Planning	Defined as: Determining a process for solving a problem. Also known as *designing.*	Differentiating assessment: To assess this cognitive category teachers might make it easier for struggling students by asking them to explain the plan for a solution that the teacher has already worked out, or teachers might provide an organizer to help the students describe a plan for a solution. The easiest assessment method could be that the students must select the correct solution plan for a given problem. To make this assessment more challenging, the teacher might ask students to develop a plan for a real world fuzzy problem they have decided to actually solve.
6.3 Producing	Defined as: Inventing something. Also known as *constructing.*	Differentiating assessment: The best way to assess this cognitive category is to ask students to design something based on specific criteria. Teachers can scaffold this category by providing graphic organizers that outline the steps and criteria clearly. Teachers can also break the task down into checkpoints that include making sure students are on the right track. To make this assessment more challenging teachers might make it a completely open-ended and fuzzy process in which the students are completely free to invent based on criteria they determine individually or as a class.

How to Use this Book

Chapter 1 provides an overview of differentiating assessment including the six parts involved in planning differentiated assessment. Chapter 2 provides an overview of types of assessment strategies. Chapters 3 through 5 provide specific differentiated assessment strategies in readiness and learning and thinking styles. And, Chapter 6 shows how the teacher might use several types of assessment in one unit of study.

The differentiation examples are a combination of ideas from many sources including my own *Handbook on Differentiating Instruction in Middle and High School* (Northey, 2005). The outline of formative assessments, however, uses the organizational structure from Silver, Strong, and Perini (2007) because although their book focuses on strategic and research-based *instruction* rather than assessment, the lessons they describe appear to be core and strategic methods of instruction that enhance the potential for differentiating assessment. (For other examples of how to use the strategies, you might see their book, *The Strategic Teacher: Selecting the Right Research-Based Strategy for Every Lesson.*)

Summary

This chapter provides an overview of crucial issues that stress the importance of including differentiated assessment as a major part of instruction. It shows the interaction among learning, assessment, and evaluation, defines differentiated assessment, explains how teachers might use a six part process to plan differentiated assessments, and provides an overview of the new version of Bloom's Taxonomy. It is important for teachers to remember that we have moved into the 21st Century and traditional thinking about how to plan instruction and how to assess student learning is changing. If teachers make differentiating assessment a priority, their students will have a better chance of gaining access to the culture of achievement that is necessary for surviving and thriving in our global society.

Note: Some of the strategies explained in this book are from a collection of assessment ideas I have gathered as a teacher. I have made every effort to determine their sources; however, if the originators of any of them feel they need to be cited, please contact me.

2

Types and Examples of Differentiated Assessments

Theorists and practitioners describe in several ways the types of assessments teachers can use to measure student achievement. This chapter provides an overview of these ways of describing them, and it provides examples of general assessment methods. As teachers begin to plan assessments, they need to think of themselves as assessors rather than activity designers. Figure 2.1 provides guidance.

Figure 2.1. Two Different Approaches to Assessment

Thinking Like an Assessor	*Thinking Like an Activity Designer*
What would be acceptable evidence of understanding?	What activities would be interesting and engaging as we learn about this topic?
What types of performance tasks will anchor the unit and focus the students' work?	What resources and materials do I have and need to teach this topic?
How can I tell who is really learning this versus who seems to be learning it?	What assignments will I give, homework and class work?
What criteria will I use to judge students' work?	How will I grade students and justify those grades to their parents?
What misunderstandings might students have and how can I check for them?	Did the activities work?

Adapted from Wiggins & McTighe (1998), p. 68.

Evaluation of Student Learning

The information in Figure 2.1 falls into the area of assessment, but what about evaluation? At what point do teachers decide what is acceptable evidence of learning, and what should they do with that evidence? Determining acceptable evidence that students have learned is a serious consideration, and teachers should take care to know when and why they are assessing what students know, what they can do, and what their attitudes are about their learning. Trussell-Cullen (1998) offers this excellent idea to help us decide some important questions about assessment. He proposes an "assessment audit" (Figure 2.2) that may help us develop a realistic perspective about the purpose(s) of assessments or evaluations of students' achievement in school.

Figure 2.2. Assessment Audit

Who is the test for?	What do they need the information for?	What kind of information do they need?
Teachers should have a clear idea of which stakeholders will be interested in the results of assessments. For most teachers stakeholders include students, parents, principals, district officials, and policy makers. The teacher is also included in this list.	This is an important question because different stakeholders may want assessments for varying reasons.	Once teachers have the answers to the first two questions, they can begin to determine the kinds of assessments to use and how they might organize and explain the results for the benefit of students.

Strategic Teaching: Assessments

Silver, Strong, & Perini (2007) have a model for differentiating instruction that includes five types of learning strategies to meet various learners' needs. These strategies include: mastery strategies, interpersonal strategies, understanding strategies, self-expression strategies, and four-style strategies. Figure 2.3 is a chart that focuses on the assessment aspect of the strategies they explain. In Chapters 3 through 5, teachers will learn specific examples of some of these strategies.

Figure 2.3. Model of Strategic Teaching—Silver, Strong, & Perini (2007)

Strategy	*Assessment*
Mastery Strategies	
New American lecture is a revision of the old lecture method that includes brain-based interactions that promote retention of concepts covered. (Ausubel, 1963, 1968)	The teacher stops at least every five minutes to ask questions that require a different style of thought. Teachers pose a problem that requires students to synthesize their learning from the lecture, assign a project, or use a traditional comprehension test.
Direct instruction is a four-phase process that results in independent learning. (updated Madeline Hunter by Robin Hunter, 2004)	The four phases are: modeling, direct practice, guided practice, and independent practice. This process encourages students to practice what they are learning without being afraid of grades. The teacher may assess students as they learn.
Graduated difficulty is a way to differentiate based on readiness. (Mosston, 1972)	The teacher designs tasks that are leveled: easy, medium, and hard. Students choose the level of difficulty and self-assess for mastery. Teachers may assess students' choices and movement toward mastery.
Teams-games-tournaments— Students compete with same-level students by answering questions to earn points for their home group. (DeVries, Edwards, & Slaven, 1978)	Teachers or students create question and answer cards that reflect the core ideas for reviewing a unit. They divide the students into heterogeneous home groups that include low, medium, and high students. Students prepare each other for the competition. Teachers assess the growth of individuals and groups.

Understanding Strategies	
Compare and contrast—Using various graphic organizers, show how various concepts and ideas are similar or different. (Marzano, Pickering, & Pollack, 2001)	Strategy includes four phases. Students: (1) Observe or read, (2) compare using a graphic organizer, (3) draw conclusions about comparisons, and (4) apply learning about comparisons. Assess at stages 2, 3, 4.
Reading for meaning—Using prereading, active reading, and postreading processes aid reading comprehension. (Herber, 1970)	Involves at least 10 types of reading strategies: vocabulary, determining main idea, inferring, forming claims or making a case, visualizing, making connections, exploring metaphor and symbol, attending to author's style, empathizing, and developing perspective. Assessment could be oral or written.
Concept attainment includes determining similarities and differences and testing hypotheses. (Bruner, 1973)	Teachers choose a concept for students to explore. They decide what examples fit into "yes," and which ones fit "no," to infer the critical attributes of the concept. Assessment includes products or tasks that show students' understanding of the concept.
Mystery—Students solve a problem or address a task by evaluating and using clues. Problem-based learning is a type of mystery learning. (Suchman, 1966)	Teachers determine a problem or task and clues that address a solution. Students make hypotheses that help solve the problem or complete the task. Assessment includes students' presentations of findings and solutions.

Self-Expression Strategies	
Inductive learning is a brainstorming and predicting process that includes grouping, labeling, and generalizing to construct central ideas. (Taba, 1971)	Teachers determine a possible generalization that they want students to discover through inductive reasoning. Assessment includes students completing a task demonstrating their understanding of the generalization.
Metaphorical expression— Students make meaning through a creative process of comparison. Other sources call this *synectics*. (Gordon, 1961)	Teachers introduce the central metaphor and then facilitate the students in developing a personal analogy, examining compressed conflicts, and extending their analogies. Assessment can be writing, developing a project, or other synthesis of the process.
Pattern maker (also known as *extrapolation*) is a way to help students see the way ideas and texts are structured or organized so that they might use those structures to create or problem solve. (Gick & Holyoak, 1980)	Teachers introduce the analogue (information source of a pattern), help students see its pattern(s), and then help students apply that pattern to new material. Assessment would include determining how well students accurately identify the structure of the analogue and apply that understanding to solve a problem or create a product.
Mind's eye—Students visualize text to help them make predictions that they test with a text. It facilitates deep understanding of a text. Alternative is visualing to problem solve. (Keene & Zimmerman, 1997)	Teachers tell students they will make movies in their minds as a text is read. Teachers then ask students to draw a picture, ask a question, make a prediction, or describe a feeling as an end product. Next teachers read 20 to 30 preselected words or phrases from the text slowly and with feeling. Assessment is the product (picture, question, etc.) and students' ability to compare that product to what they find in the text.

Interpersonal Strategies	
Reciprocal learning—Students coach each other through the process of learning new information. Learning is doubled through this process. (Silver, Strong, & Perini, 2007)	Teachers create a reciprocal learning assignment and break students into pairs with one being A and the other, B. Teachers model the coaching process, and then troubleshoot while one student coaches the other one as he or she completes half of the assignment or a separate one, and then they switch roles. Assessment is the completion of the assignment and each student's ability to demonstrate successful coaching.
Decision making—Students get "inside" topics when the teacher asks them to make decisions about it. (Silver, Strong, & Perini, 2007)	Teachers set up a situation that requires students to make decisions and then help them identify sources of information, develop criteria, and decide how to communicate their decisions. Assessment is the quality of that communication.
Jigsaw is a cooperative learning strategy in which students read and report to their home group on a part of a reading task. (Aronson, Blaney, Stephen, Sikes, & Snapp, 1978)	Teachers determine an assignment (usually reading), divide students into cooperative home groups, and have groups number off. All the ones (twos, etc.) read the same part of the assignment and then talk about how to communicate what they learned to their home group. Assessment of learning from jigsaw can be a test on the materials.
Community circle helps students build a sense of community as they learn about themselves through sharing their thoughts, feelings, and values. (Silver, Strong, & Perini, 2007)	Assessment occurs when teachers help students reflect on what came out in the discussion. Students self-assess and give helpful feedback (nonjudgmental) to each other.

Four-Style Strategies	
Window notes expand the process of note taking to include not only the facts about a topic, but also the students' feelings, questions, and ideas about that topic. (Silver, Strong, & Perini, 2007)	Teachers ask students to divide a sheet of paper into four sections and label them as follows: facts, feelings, questions, ideas. When students read something, they make notes including information for each of the sections. Assessment is the teacher's evaluation of the notes.
Circle of Knowledge, also known as Socratic Seminar if it is text-based, is a strategy that promotes academic discussion. (Silver, Strong, & Perini, 2007)	Teachers ask students to discuss a topic in a scholarly manner. Assessment can be a method of crediting students for making high-quality remarks about the topic, and for Socratic Seminar, referencing the text, which is a great method for oral language practice including use of standard English.
Do you hear what I hear? Students listen to teacher read a selection of information and then respond to what they heard (Strong, Silver, Perini, & Tuculescu, 2002).	Teachers choose a selection of information to read to the class. Students just listen to the first reading, and then take notes on the second reading. Assessment is students showing what they know from what they heard in a variety of products or performances.
Task rotation—Students choose from a variety of mastery, understanding, self-expression, or interpersonal tasks. (Silver, Strong, & Perini, 2007)	Teachers determine a variety of tasks from which students can choose to show what they have learned. Assessment is differentiated naturally because students can choose how they want to show what they know.

Adapted from *The Strategic Teacher: Selecting the Right Research-Based Strategy for Every Lesson,* by H. Silver, W. Strong, & M. Perini, 2007, Alexandria, VA: Association for Supervision and Curriculum Development.

Types of Assessments

Practitioners and theorists often refer to three types of assessment: preassessment, formative assessment, and summative assessment. I have added informal and affective assessment. Figure 2.4 is an overview of how they are evaluated, when they are used, and their major purposes.

Figure 2.4. Five Types of Assessments

Type	Grading/ Evaluating	When Used	Purpose
Preassessment	A check mark for participation: + = high quality; – = low quality	Before learning	1. Lets teachers know what their students already understand, know, and can do related to the topic or concept. 2. Helps teachers decide what they need to include in their unit. 3. Piques students' interest in the unit.
Informal assessment	A check mark for participation: + = high quality; – = low quality	During learning	1. Allows teachers to take whole class and individual assessments that are quick and easy to note. 2. These assessments can evaluate cognitive or affective growth.
Formative assessment	Can be a check mark with pluses and minuses or A, B, and N (for "needs work" or "not yet")	During learning	1. Helps teachers adjust their instruction so that students have a better chance of learning. 2. Allows teachers to constantly check to see what their students understand, know, and can do. 3. Provides an opportunity for teachers to give students clear and comprehensive feedback on their learning to date.

Type	Grading/ Evaluating	When Used	Purpose
Summative assessment	Grades such as A,B,C, D. & F or "Not Yet" or "Needs work"	After learning	Allows teachers and students to know how successful they were when the unit is completed. May help teachers adjust instruction for the future and may provide information that suggests remediation for students.
Affective assessment	Not graded Sutdents write reflections in "Learning Logs" that the teacher reads and checks off	Before, during, and after learning	*Answers these questions:* How interesting is this topic to each student? What do students believe and feel about what they have learned? How does this learning affect students as learners? Provides teachers constant access to how students are reacting emotionally to the unit. Assess often.

Keeping these ideas in mind, the following sections are some examples of assessments that would fit any situation in any content.

Preassessments: Literacy Readiness

One of the most important things a middle or high school teacher needs to know about his or her students is how literate each student is in the subject area the teacher is teaching them. Not only do teachers need to know how well students can read and understand the major materials (usually a textbook) the teacher uses to teach the class, they also need to know how well students have incorporated the core structures and protocols of that subject area. [See Northey (2005) for several ways to assess students' reading level.] Teachers may use standardized test results to help them determine reading levels, or if they have reasons to believe the student may not be able to read at grade level, they may refer the student for a thorough reading assessment. If the school uses "Accelerated Reader," teachers can use the "Star Test" to determine students' lexile levels. The teacher may want to take some time with individual students to get a good idea for how well that student reads. Sometimes the teacher is surprised that students read their text so poorly. If the teacher knows a student has difficulty reading a text independently, he or she must find alternative materials or provide significant scaffolding to help the student access the text.

Reading Aloud

It is critical that teachers know how well students can read the materials from which they teach. Teachers often use round-robin reading as a classroom management tool or as a way to assure that everyone in the class is reading and understanding the text. Brain-based research and other reading research tell us that round-robin reading is an ineffective reading method. The most compelling reason, among many others, is that according to brain-based research, when students are reading aloud, the area in the brain that is comprehending the text (making meaning) is in competition with the parts of the brain that are controlling speaking and other physiological aspects that occur when a student reads aloud. In other words, it is difficult for students to read aloud and comprehend what they are reading. Also, depending on the reading ability of the student reading aloud, especially his or her fluency, the students who are listening may not be able to comprehend the text. There are many other wonderful methods of oral reading and shared reading that teachers might use. Here are two excellent titles: *Good-bye Round Robin: 25 Effective Oral Reading Strategies* by Michael Opitz and Timothy Rasinski (1998) and *Strategies for Integrating Reading and Writing* by Karen Wood (2001).

Preassessments: Learning Styles

When teachers plan to differentiate assessment, they need to have a full range of learning styles inventories from which to choose. See my books, *Handbook on Differentiating Instruction in Middle and High School* (Northey, 2005) and *The Democratic Differentiated Classroom* (Waterman, 2007) for several learning styles inventories. See Chapter 1 for an overview of learning and thinking styles.

Preassessments: Interests

Assessing interest in a topic can be a matter of asking students in a short survey about their interest in a specific part of a unit of study and in the unit of study as a whole. The survey could be as simple as asking the following:

◆ Rate your interest in this topic from 1 (no interest) to 10 (very interested).

◆ If you are not very interested in this topic, what would make you more interested in it? Please be specific.

Knowing if students have a fundamental interest or disinterest in the topic can help teachers adjust assessments so that motivation is optimal.

Preassessments: Content

Anticipation Guide (Herber, 1978)

Many textbooks have interesting true/false guides in their ancillary resources, but teachers can also construct these for any unit or topic. The teacher writes a few (no more than 10) statements that could be true or false about the unit or topic. Students make their best guess to determine if the statements are true or false. After students have made their best guesses, they read the source of information and correct their misconceptions. This guide can create curiosity and motivation to read for understanding.

Five Question Preassessment Quiz

This is a great way to start a unit and to engage students in a unit of study. The teacher chooses five questions that might pique students' interest in a topic and might give the teacher a good idea of what they already know about it. The discussion that follows this preassessment quiz, if handled correctly, can get any unit off to an exciting start.

KWL (Adaptation) (Ogle, 1986)

Teachers who use this strategy should make a chart with a big K for what we already know, W for what we want to learn, and L for how we want to learn. This is a perfect strategy for teachers to learn the extent of some of the students' background knowledge of a topic. The teacher needs to keep in mind, however, that just because one or more students place an idea in the K box does not mean that all students have that K. The W is an excellent place to help students learn to develop essential questions (EQs) for the unit. The L helps the teachers know how certain members of the class want to learn about the topic. This information is also helpful for designing formative assessments.

The teacher might also adapt the KWL to help gather important information about what individual students know and can do regarding the topic of a unit of study. To use this method most effectively the teacher should know what skills are required to learn about the topic, and what skills students might learn or develop as they explore the unit. The teacher should also have a clear idea of the knowledge students will gain by exploring this unit.

It is also important that students prove they can do the things they say they can do, and that they know the things they say they know. In addition to the survey, therefore, the teacher should also include a sample problem attached to the pretest and a typical problem attached to the posttest. These sample problems will verify that students can in fact do what they say they can do and that they know what they say they know.

By preassessing and postassessing, the teacher and student will have a better idea about the learning that took place. The students might actually count the number of skills and knowledge they listed before and after studying the unit, thus quantifying the amount of learning. They could also use a rating scale to quantify attitudes, interests, and feelings.

Figure 2.5. Know and Do Pre- and Post-Assessment

Adaptation of the KWL

Name: _____ Date:_____

Topic of Unit: _____

1. I know how to:

    (Complete this stem by listing skills related to learning about this unit of study.)

2. How many ideas did you list?_____

3. I know that:

    (Complete this stem by listing information and ideas you know about this unit of study.)

4. How many ideas did you list?_____

5. Write one or two sentences explaining your general knowledge about and interest in this unit of study.

6. Rate your general knowledge and interest in this unit of study (1 being lowest and 10 being highest): _____

7. Write one or two sentences explaining how you feel about exploring this unit of study.

8. Rate your feelings about exploring this unit of study (1 being lowest and 10 being highest):
    Total score:_

9. Complete the assignment attached to this form.

Keeping Track of Learning

Students might track their learning for the year using the format in Figure 2.6.

Figure 2.6. Track My Learning

Tracking My Learning in_____ for School Year_____ Write the title of each unit of study in the spaces below. Record the dates of study in the appropriate boxes. Record your total score (from your preassessment and post-assessment from your Know and Do Pre- and Post-Assessment forms) in the appropriate boxes.			
Title of Unit of Study	**Dates of Study**	**Prescore**	**Post-Score**
Looking at this quantitative measure of your learning over the year, what conclusions can you draw?			

3-2-1

The teacher might preassess what students already know, what they want to learn, and any other information by using a 3-2-1 activity. The teacher may also use this strategy as a summative assessment. To use it as a preassessment, the teacher may give students an index card or ask them to write the information on their own paper and then ask them to list the following:

♦ 3 things you want to learn about this topic

♦ 2 questions you have about it

♦ 1 way you want to learn about it (i.e., writing, researching, group activities, etc.)

Quick Write (Rief, 1998)

To preassess what students already know about a topic, the teacher might ask them to write (without stopping) for 5 to 10 minutes about the topic. The teacher might also use this with a partner. For instance the teacher asks the students to write everything they know about at topic and then exchange papers with a partner. Following this exercise, the teacher may then ask partners to share at least one important idea they already know about the topic.

Interview

The teacher might give students an interview template and ask them to find out what at least three students in the class already know about the topic. They might then turn the template in so that the teacher can get a better idea about what students already know. Students can also take turns sharing what they found out in their interviews.

Informal Assessments

Informal assessments are defined here as quick checks for understanding that the teacher can use without a great deal of preparation or development of an instrument. The two major types of informal assessments are (1) pop or announced, short written quizzes and (2) oral or other impromptu quickly written checks for understanding at the beginning, middle, or end of classroom instruction. Informal assessments are great ways to determine if all students are learning *while* the teacher is instructing them. If the teacher does not have a good idea of how students are learning on a daily basis, he or she may inadvertently move forward and leave one, several, or the majority of the class behind.

Pop or Announced Short Written Quizzes

Five-Question Quiz to Start or End the Class

If the teacher uses a quick written quiz as an informal assessment to check if students have understood and retained the information addressed in the lesson, there are a few ideas to consider as follows:

♦ Use a five-question quiz based on the essential ideas of the previous or current day's lesson. These questions should capture the critical concepts included in the lesson. They should be questions that teachers can quickly determine and with which they may be flexible depending on what they in fact were able to cover in the lesson.

♦ The teacher could grade the quiz as follows: A+ for all correct, A– for one missed, B for two missed, C for three missed, D for four missed, and F for all missed.

◆ The teacher may count these as quiz grades (not weighted) or may use them to learn if students have gaps in their understanding of concepts.

◆ The teacher should collect the quizzes in a predetermined amount of time, not allowing students to use more time than allotted. They will get use to the idea that the teacher is timing the quiz, and they know the information or they don't. Giving this kind of informal assessment is a great way to settle and quiet a class in the beginning and at the end of the class.

◆ The five-question quiz fits well into any lesson plan because teachers may use it for review at the beginning or end of any class.

Oral or Other Impromptu Checks for Understanding

According to Fisher and Frey (2007), oral assessment is a wonderful way to check for understanding; however, there are several issues to consider when using this kind of informal assessment: "poverty, language, and perceived skill level; gender differences; and the initiate-respond-evaluate (IRE) model of questioning" (p. 21). Fisher and Frey (2007) cite several studies that show the following: Teachers do most of the talking in all classes, but they do even more talking in classes of at-risk students.

◆ Teachers call on girls less and less as they get older. They call on boys more often and ask them higher-level questions.

◆ The IRE model that has been in teachers' practices for years is ineffective because it does not focus on critical thinking for *all* students. It goes like this: I—teacher asks a question, R—students try to guess the answer the teacher is looking for, and E—the teacher makes an evaluative statement, such as, "great answer" or "no, that is not correct."

The following sections offer strategies and solutions to these problems identified by Fisher and Frey (2007, pp. 21–35).

Noticing Nonverbal Cues

Remembering that much of our communication is nonverbal, teachers can be alert to the looks on students' faces and other nonverbal cues to help them informally assess learning. Some students may be too shy to call attention to their misunderstanding; however, if the teacher notices a puzzled look on a student's face, he or she might provide a less embarrassing way for the student to get clarification.

Whip Around

Fisher and Frey (2007) suggest that "Whip Around" is a great informal way to find out if a group of students is following the instruction and what misconceptions or gaps might exist in their learning. Here is how it goes:

1. At the end of instruction, the teacher asks students a question that might have at least three parts to the answer, or the teacher asks students to list at least three things they learned about the lesson.

2. The teacher asks students to write their three things on a scrap piece of paper.

3. The teacher then tells students to stand up when they have finished writing their three things. He or she tells them that when they have heard all the items on their scrap of paper mentioned, they should sit down.

4. Next, the teacher calls on one student at a time to read one of the items on their scrap of paper.

5. The teacher tells students that if they hear an item they have listed, they should cross it off their list, but that they should remain standing until at least one student has mentioned the item.

6. The teacher continues to call on students until all are seated.

By following this process, the teacher can note any significant ideas that students left out.

Whole-Class Hand Signals

A way to check to see if all students understand, know, or can do some aspect of a topic or concept is through hand signals.

Method One

Students answer a question or work a problem. The teacher instructs students to do the following:

1. Put a fist in front of your chest.

2. Indicate agreement with the answer or solution by putting a thumb up, indicate disagreement with the answer or solution by putting a thumb down, and indicate ambivalence with the answer or solution by making the hand wiggle back and forth.

Method Two

The teacher asks a question with A, B, C, or D as answers

1. Put a fist in front of the chest.

2. Indicate the correct letter using American Sign Language to designate A, B, C, or D.

Method Three: Seven Hands Raised

After a teacher asks a question, she says she will not get an answer until seven people have raised their hands. She then calls on one of them to answer (Smith, 2004).

Waiting until seven hands are raised does two things: (1) forces wait time and (2) assures that more students are taking responsibility for oral assessment.

Method Four

The teacher asks students to close their eyes and then to rate their understanding of the lesson as follows: 3 = excellent understanding, 2 = moderate understanding, and 1 = poor understanding. She asks students to hold up their hands when the teacher calls the number of their rating. For instance, when the teacher calls out 3, all students who have an excellent grasp on the lesson will raise their hands (Allen, 2007).

An adaptation of this method is that students should put a 1, 2, or 3 in front of their bodies to show how well they have understood the lesson.

Whole Class Movement

Four Corners

The teacher asks a question and gives four possible answers. Each answer is assigned a corner of the room. Students go to the corner with which they agree.

White-Board Assessments

Students use a marker to work a problem or answer a question on a small white board.

Method One

Students work individually or with a partner.
1. The teacher asks a question or states a problem.
2. Students record their answers on the white board with a marker.
3. When the teacher says, "hold up your answer," each student holds up the white board with his or her answer on it.

Method Two

Students work individually or with a partner.
1. The teacher assigns each person or partners a sentence to write, problem to work, or other.
2. Students record their work on a white board.
3. Students share their work as a presentation before the class.
4. Class members put thumbs up or thumbs down to assess agreement or disagreement with students' solutions.

Method Three

The teacher might use a new technology that provides handheld small white boards of slates on which students might record answers that can be uploaded onto a large white board at the front of the class.

Demand Response

Names in Basket

Teachers get a small basket for each of their classes and put each student's name in it. The teacher asks a question and pulls a name out of the basket to decide on whom to call. A standard follow-up question, "Why is that your answer?" takes the process automatically to a higher level of thinking.

The following are ways to differentiate demand response for struggling students:

♦ Allow them to "phone a friend"

♦ Ask an opinion question

♦ Preview the question and its answer in a "secret" conversation

♦ Ask a struggling student to share his or her answer when you have walked around and noticed that he or she has written a good answer

♦ Call on a student when you know he or she has a good answer even if you have not actually pulled his or her name. No one knows whose name is really being pulled.

♦ Acccept "I don't know the answer *yet*," and then prompt the student to figure it out.

Formative Assessments

Using Formative Assessments to Prepare Students for Standardized Tests

Many teachers make faulty assumptions about the best way to prepare students to take standardized tests during which students must read a selection and answer multiple-choice questions. They believe the best way to prepare students to take these tests is to use an outside source of reading selections (many varied reading selections are provided online or published in test-preparation books) that help them simulate the testing process. They ask students to read selections, answer the questions, and then go over the answers as a class. An alternative to this method includes the following two ideas:

1. Teachers can learn to write the kinds of questions that may be used on standardized tests. They should go online to obtain a list of question stems on

which their district or state bases its curriculum. They can then use their own content as selections for multiple-choice testing assessments. Teachers should make sure that deep learning is the goal and that using multiple-choice questions aligned with standardized tests are for building skill with these kinds of questions. Teachers might also give students stems from which to compose their own questions that align with standardized tests.

2. Teachers could use outside sources for reading selections; however, instead of asking students to read, and then immediately answer standardized questions, the teacher could use an instructional strategy or formative assessment to help students better understand the selection. Here is a general list of possible formative assessment activities:

- Make a diagram of the plot or organizational style of the selection.

- Make a cause and effect graphic organizer.

- Draw pictures of various aspects of the selection that show comprehension.

- Use Venn diagrams or other compare and contrast graphic organizers to make sure students understand the selection.

- Use thinking maps, charts, or organizers to show reading comprehension.

- Use outlining.

- Use a "fact trap" to determine main idea and supporting details (Figure 2.7). From Patricia Gregory, "EOG Reading," Workshop, February 15, 2008.

Figure 2.7. Fact Trap

Supporting Details	Main Idea	Supporting Details

To make test preparation more like a learning process than *"skill and drill," teachers should use any assessment strategy that helps students comprehend the selection before moving to answering the standardized questions.* From Patricia Gregory, "EOG Reading," Workshop, February 15, 2008.

Cooperative Learning Formative Assessments

Cooperative learning activities can help teachers determine if individual students are learning; however, they must take special care to design assessments that provide individual data. Although cooperative learning activities should be interdependent, it is dangerous to give grades to individuals based on the work of the group. Teachers can, however, use various techniques to capitalize on group solidarity to inspire all members of the group to achieve. Here are helpful guidelines from Sagor and Cox (2004) on developing cooperative learning activities.

Step 1: The teacher decides what objective(s) to address and describes the product that will address that objective.

Step 2: The teacher decides why he or she wants to use cooperative learning.

Step 3: The teacher determines the roles that each person will have in each cooperative group.

Step 4: The teacher designs a method for individual accountability.

Figure 2.8 shows a few specific ideas about how to differentiate assessments from cooperative learning activities.

Figure 2.8. Differentiate Assessments from Cooperative Learning Activities

Structure	How to Do It	Differentiated Assessment Strategies
Numbered Heads Together (Kagen, 1997)	Students form small groups of four or five. The teacher asks questions, and the students consult with each other to decide on the answer. One student provides the answer.	1. The teacher makes the groups homogeneous based on similar academic achievement. 2. Specially differentiated questions are asked of each group. 3. Each student receives a participation check. 4. Quality designations are awarded (+ for exceptional and – for needs work)
Think-Pair-Share (Kagen, 1997)	The teacher poses a question or situation. Students are asked to think about it for a short time. Next, students find a partner to share what they have thought. Finally, the teacher asks for answers.	1. This is a great way to differentiate assessment and use the findings of brain-based research, which states that students learn best when they are not in a stressful situation. By allowing struggling students to discuss their thinking with another student, the teacher is greatly reducing the stress they might feel if they had to find the answers alone. 2. This is also a great way to capitalize on the idea that students learn from each other.
Pairs Check (Kagen, 1997)	Students form groups of four. Within that group, two students work as partners to solve problems. One works the problem while the other coaches. After every two problems, the pairs check to see if they have the same answers. Students may reverse roles or stay the same.	As with Think-Pair-Share this is a good stress reducer and a chance for students to learn from each other. It works nicely as a formative assessment because the teacher can tell if students understand how to solve the problems. Teachers might also use this strategy for answering questions on an assignment sheet.

Oral Formative Assessments

"Accountable Talk"

Teachers might improve oral assessments if they use a strategy cited in Fisher and Frey (2007) called "Accountable Talk," which was developed by Lauren Resnick (2000). It includes a list of agreements teachers and students make concerning student to student conversations. "Accountable Talk" includes the following three requirements that students learn, practice, and agree to maintain:

1. Staying on topic
2. Using information that is accurate and appropriate
3. Listening carefully and thinking about what others say

Accountable talk also requires students to follow these strategies that they learn, practice, and maintain for each non-teacher-led discussion:

1. Press the speaker to clarify and explain. "Could you describe what you mean?"
2. Require the speaker to justify proposals or challenges to others' proposals by referencing the source. "Where did you find that information?"
3. Challenge ideas that seem wrong "I don't agree because…"
4. Require the speaker to provide evidence for claims. "Can you give me an example?"
5. Use each other's statements. "Susan suggested… and I agree with her."

Values Lineup

Values lineup developed by Kagen and cited in Fisher and Frey (2007) is an excellent method for orally assessing how students feel about an academic topic. It also helps them practice expressing themselves orally. It goes like this:

1. The teacher prepares a statement or statements that represent the essential concepts of an academic topic.
2. Students evaluate the statement and position themselves in a line according to that evaluation (levels of agreement or disagreement).
3. The teacher then asks the students to fold the line in half so that the students at either ends of the continuum will talk to one another.

Retellings

Another great way to find out orally if students understand what they are reading is to use the process of retelling. To use this strategy, the teacher needs to teach students by doing the following:

1. Explain that retelling is the process of recreating a text in your own words.

2. Help students see that retelling something they have read in school is similar to telling a friend about a movie they have seen.

3. Model for students how to retell a piece of text.

4. Discuss with students the differences and similarities between the retelling and the actual text.

5. Select another text and ask students to practice retelling.

6. Once again compare the differences and similarities between the original text and the retelling.

According to Fisher and Frey (2007) there are many types of retelling as follows: oral to oral, oral to written, oral to video, reading to oral, reading to written, reading to video, viewing to oral, viewing to writing, viewing to video. Fisher and Frey also include a rubric for retellings in their book (2007, p. 29).

Assessment Tools

This section includes an overview of types of tools for evaluating student work, such as the following: rubrics, constructing multiple-choice tests, participation grid, portfolios.

Rubrics

Using and Designing Effective Rubrics

Teachers may easily go online to find a website that will help them design a rubric for any assessment they may be planning. Rubrics are excellent tools to evaluate a differentiated assessment of students' learning. There are two basic kinds of rubrics, analytical and holistic. Analytical rubrics break the description of the levels of performance into discrete parts whereas holistic rubrics list the parts as one whole statement or paragraph. One might use an analytical rubric for formative evaluation and a holistic rubric for summative evaluation. The best kind of rubric from my perspective is a "consensus rubric" (Waterman, 2007). This kind of rubric allows teachers to determine with the class what constitutes quality work. Here are the steps to working with students to design a consensus rubric:

Step 1: The teacher arranges the room in a circle if possible. Rows may work, but students will have a harder time talking to one another.

Step 2: The teacher hands each student a copy of the blank rubric chart (Figure 2.9) and tells them that the class will be working together to plan a consensus rubric.

Step 3: The teacher asks students to work alone or with a partner to determine categories for evaluating a certain assessment.

Step 4: The teacher asks students to share their ideas about categories with the whole class.

Step 5: The teacher should use voting to decide the top four categories. Some typical categories may be as follows: originality, content, organization, or technical quality.

Step 6: After the teacher has decided those categories, he or she should ask students this question: "What does a 4 look like?" He or she might start with the highest quality but could start anywhere. The class continues filling in the rubric until it is complete.

Note: The first time the class does this, the teacher may need to directly instruct and model for students what constitutes the most appropriate evaluative words and phrases. One way to do this is to analyze the words and phrases professional rubric-makers use.

Figure 2.9. How to Create a Consensus Rubric

Materials needed: (1) a blank rubric chart like this:

Category	Level 1	Level 2	Level 3	Level 4

One of the challenges with using rubrics is converting their scores to grades. Here is how to do it. For an analytical rubric, the teacher should give each category a point value. For instance in any rubric, each category could be worth 25 points each, or teachers could weight the points in some way, such as 20 points for writing, 20 points for organization, 50 points for accuracy, and 10 points for graphics. They should deduct points for each category based on the student's attainment of the rubric standards.

For example, for a "brochure project," Jane's brochure has the following features:

◆ For "writing/organization," each section has an exceptionally clear and thoughtful beginning, middle, and end. Score 25 points.

◆ For "attractiveness/organization," the brochure has attractive formatting, but it is not exceptional. There is one place that it is somewhat sloppy. Deduct 5 points. Score 20.

◆ For "content/accuracy," the student has made one error in accuracy. Deduct 1 point. Score 24.

◆ For "graphics/pictures," there are too many graphics and not enough text; however, the graphics do go with the text and there is one original graphic. Deduct 11 points. Score 14.

Scores are as follows:

Writing/organization	25
Attractiveness/organization	20
Content/accuracy	24
Graphics/pictures	14
Total score	83 = C or C+

For the holistic rubric the teacher could use the following scoring process:

4 = no loss of points = A+
3 = loss of 1–11 points = 89–99 = A, A–, or B+
2 = loss of 12–23 points = 88–77 = B, C+, or C
1 = loss of 24 or more points = 76–0 = D+, D, D–, or F

Or the teacher can say that Level 4 = A (well above average); Level 3 = B (above average); Level 2 = C (average); Level 1 = D (below average); and not doing the work at all is F or Not Yet.

Some systems consider 2 to be failing (below average) and 1 to be well below average. Also as mentioned previously, it is a good policy to avoid zeroes.

Designing rubrics has become quite easy with all the online sources available. The teacher might also encourage students to explore these rubric-making sites. Figure 2.10 is an annotated list of some of the best ones teachers may use.

Figure 2.10. Rubric-Making Websites

Website and Address	Description
RubiStar http://Rubistar.4teachers.org	A free tool to help teachers create excellent rubrics. Easy to use and comprehensive.
Teachnology: *The Web Portal for Educators* http://www.teach-nology.com/	Has free rubric-maker capacity for a wide variety of topics from behavior modification to evaluating oral projects.
Kathy Schrock's Guide for Educators http://schooldiscovery.com/schrockguide/assess.html.	Has excellent subject-specific and general rubrics and web-based rubrics that include assessing WebQuests, school web pages, classroom web pages, and student web pages.
Midlink Magazine Teacher Tools http://www.ncsu.edu/midlink/ho.html	Has a wide variety of multimedia rubrics, software evaluation rubrics, and many more.

Summative Assessment Tools—Tests

Most textbooks provide summative assessments for teachers to use; however, *it might be best for teachers to create their own unit tests based on their standard course of study and based on students' needs.* To construct a "fair" summative assessment for students, teachers might evaluate their assessment based on the following checklist (Figure 2.11). The idea of a checklist comes from Linn and Miller as cited in Fisher and Frey (2007). I have adapted their adaptation of Linn and Miller. See Fisher and Frey (2007) for a more thorough discussion of these kinds of assessments. Figures 2.11 through 2.16 are a series of possible checklists teachers might use to evaluate their assessments.

Figure 2.11. General Criteria

Check	Criteria
_____	I have picked a test that matches the way I taught this topic.
_____	I am assessing the essential knowledge and skills for this topic.
_____	My test does not require my students to read at a level that might prevent their showing me what they actually know and understand.
_____	There are no typos or mistakes in my test that would confuse students.
_____	My test does a good job of being culturally relevant and unbiased for my students.
_____	I have prepared my students for this test so that they should be adequately challenged, but not overwhelmed by it.
_____	The directions for taking the test are clear and easy to understand.

True/False Tests

To make these kinds of assessments fair, teachers should make sure they can check off these criteria:

Figure 2.12. True -False Tests

Check	Criteria
_____	The statements are only true or false, not partially true in some cases and false in others.
_____	The statements are appropriately challenging.
_____	The statements do not address opinions.
_____	The statements are similar in length.
_____	The statements include no double negatives.
_____	Each statement includes only one fact.

True/false questions are problematic because of guessing, which most students are accustomed to doing. One way to solve that problem is to require students to correct statements they believe are false.

Short Answer

To make these kinds of assessments fair for students, teachers should make sure they can check off these criteria:

Figure 2.13. Short Answer Questions

Check	Criteria
_____	The answers include a symbol, word, or phrase.
_____	The question does not give clues to the answer (such as an, a).
_____	The questions are in student-friendly language for at-risk students.
_____	The test leaves space for showing work.

Multiple Choice

To make these kinds of assessments fair for students, teachers should make sure they can check off these criteria:

Figure 2.14. Multiple Choice Tests

Check	Criteria
_____	The item stems are aligned with the objectives of the unit and with district or state curriculum standards.
_____	The item stems reflect a continuum of thinking skills.
_____	The stems are written in positive terms.
_____	The distracters are similar in length and style to the true answers.
_____	The items do not give clues to the correct answer.
_____	The stems are clear, specific, and unambiguous.

Matching

To make these kinds of assessments fair, teachers should make sure they can check off these criteria:

Figure 2.15. Matching

Check   **Criteria**

_____ The test does not include more than approximately 20 items.

_____ The test is all on one page.

_____ There is one match for each statement.

_____ I have taken the test myself to make sure everything matches.

This is a low-level testing process because the content must be based on facts to be successful.

Extended Writing Response

To make these kinds of assessments fair, teachers should make sure they can check off these criteria:

Figure 2.16. Extended Writing Response

Check   **Criteria**

_____ Students understand how I will evaluate the writing.

_____ Students know how much time they have to write their response.

_____ The writing prompt addresses higher-level thinking processes.

_____ The writing allows at-risk students to be successful even if their writing skills are weak.

_____ I have given students writing choices. (This is not mandatory, but it is a good idea.)

_____ I have written the response myself so I have some idea what students will write or should write.

Constructing Multiple-Choice Tests

Standardized tests are a current reality, and they have usually functioned as the primary gateway into colleges and universities; therefore, teachers must not ignore the importance of teaching their students the strategy of identifying best answers in multiple-choice tests (i.e., convergent reasoning). Teachers often have access to multiple-choice tests formats provided for them by their districts or provided in test-preparation workbooks; however, teachers can greatly increase their capability of providing multiple-choice question answering practice for their students by doing two things.

- ♦ Learning how to write high-level multiple-choice questions based on text-books and other print and nonprint resources
- ♦ Teaching students to write high-level multiple-choice questions themselves

Teachers Writing Their Own Tests

What follows are some steps that might help teachers write their own multiple-choice questions.

Step 1: Teachers should analyze the types of multiple-choice question stems standardized tests require their students to answer. They should then make a list of these stems if their school system does not provide them.

Step 2: As teachers read and go over the materials they have for their content area, they should use those stems to construct questions that address the most important aspects of their materials.

Step 3: Teachers should choose answers that for the most part *could* be true, but only one answer is *best*. These "could be true" answers are called distracters. The best kinds of distracters fall into one of these categories: misconception, oversimplification, or overgeneralization. Teachers should learn to write these distracters if they want to construct strong multiple-choice tests for their students. It is also a good idea to teach students how to write questions with appropriate distracters. This step can be tricky because questions need to be fair. Teachers should avoid questions that are based on opinion or that might reflect a bias. They should focus on questions that reflect the *best* interpretation or analysis. They should make sure they do not include more than one *correct* answer.

Step 4: Teachers should find a quick way to score these multiple-choice tests. The "bubble sheet" (see below) is a quick and easy way for students to respond to multiple-choice tests. If the school does not have bubble sheets or a scoring machine, here is how to make bubble sheets and how to score students' multiple-choice responses with one of them:

Making and Hand-Scoring a Multiple-Choice Test Bubble Sheet

Step 1: The teacher makes the test.

Step 2: Print enough copies of a "bubble sheet" for all class members and one for the key (use *Catpin.com* or other websites that construct bubble sheets).

Step 3: Teachers should take the test themselves (this will help discover any mistakes) to make the key.

Step 4: Laminate the key.

Step 5: Use a hole-puncher with a long neck or make slits down each row.

Step 6: Use a hole-puncher to punch out the correct answers on the key.

Step 7: Use a colored marker to mark students' incorrect answers on their test through the holes in the key. The teacher can quickly see how many questions students missed to determine their score.

Whole Class Oral Participation Assessments

When teachers use a whole-class oral assessment, such as a discussion group, they may want to track students' participation using the following grid (Figure 2.17). Some teachers announce student scores at the end of the discussion. Being able to announce high grades can be motivational for students but announcing low grades can have the opposite effect. Teachers may want to consider the culture of the class to decide if they want to do this.

Figure 2.17. Class Participation Grid

Student															Grade

Instructions: List all the students in the class. Put a plus sign or check mark for every positive comment a student makes in a class discussion and put a minus sign for every negative response a student makes during class discussion. Decide how many pluses or check marks constitute an A, B, C, D, or F. Deduct minuses from the total pluses or check marks.

Summary

This chapter provided several generic methods for differentiating assessment including ideas for pre-assessing, informally assessing, assessing affect, and formative and summative assessments. In the chapters that follow, teachers will see specific examples of these strategies.

3

Highly Structured Math and Science Assessments

This chapter shows teachers specific examples of differentiated assessment strategies that are leveled for students who have special readiness needs. After providing an overview of these students' special needs, it provides examples of preassessments, formative assessments, and summative assessments. For the formative assessments, it provides information about "Differentiating Assessment – Six Parts. What follows is a thorough explanation of Part I for students who might need a highly structured assessment experience.

Students' Needs

Who Are the Students Who Need a Great Deal of Structure?

Students for whom we need to provide a great deal of structure in our assessments are called "at risk," "struggling," or "priority" students. In this book, we will call them "at-risk" students because that term seems to be most descriptive. At-risk students include those who are at risk of failing, having behavior problems, or dropping out of school related to their academic readiness, motivation, or learning styles. This term can also describe students who are learning disabled and struggling English language learners. When we think about assessing them we need to consider several important factors.

One of the most critical factors involved in planning assessments for at-risk students is determining these students' level of social functioning. In addition to academic learning issues, these students can have severe social functioning limitations. They often have weaknesses in impulse control and empathy. In addition, they might not have developed past the lowest levels of ethical development so that they do not appear to have an intrinsic sense of doing what is right because it is right. They might do what is right if they fear punishment or if they think they will reap a reward. This factor leads many teachers to continue to attach the practice of reward and punishment to their assessments, which may limit students' intrinsic development of ethical behavior.

Activities, such as cooperative learning and partner sharing, can fail if the teacher lacks classroom management skills and the class is comprised of mostly or all at-risk students. What follows are some possibly useful answers from a book by Belvel and Jordan, *Rethinking Classroom Management*. Based on a study done by the U.S. Department of Labor (Carnevale et al., 1989 as cited in Belvel & Jordan, 2003), they propose that students are successful in social activities such as cooperative learning and partner work if they have attained a certain social skill level. Their chart (Belvel & Jordan, 2003, p. 87) includes four levels of social skill development that are necessary for certain kinds of classroom activities (Figure 3.1).

Figure 3.1. Levels of Social Skill Development

Level	Description
I. Connecting/ bonding skills	1. Knowing other students in the class and calling them by name 2. Making appropriate eye contact with others 3. Treating others with respect 4. Understanding it is important to stay with their group until the teacher tells them to move 5. Understanding it is important to gather and share materials 6. Cleaning up after themselves and their group 7. Solving social problems by asking authorities for help
II. Interacting skills	1. Giving ideas to others 2 Talking about their work 3. Asking relevant questions 4. Saying "Thank you" and other acceptable phrases 5. Including others in decision making 6. Actively listening when others are talking
III. Communicating skills	1. Encouraging others 2. Empathizing 3. Putting their feelings and ideas into their own words 4. Acknowledging the achievements of others 5. Appreciating the input of others 6. Contributing thought ideas to a group or partner discussion
IV. Decision-making and problem-solving skills	1. Listening respectfully to other points of view 2. Generating and implementing thoughtful solutions to identified problems 3. Redirecting the group to work on the task the teacher has assigned 4. Knowing how to use appropriate decision-making strategies 5. Knowing how to summarize for the group

If students show that they are unable to incorporate these social skills in their classroom behaviors, they most likely will not be able to successfully participate in partner or group activities. To remedy this problem, teachers should spend time establishing trusting relationships with these students, and also time training them to incorporate these social skills in their own lives. Secondary teachers often resist being teachers of behavior; however, we must realize that we are teaching the whole child or young person and that the reality is that many of them have not yet mastered the social skills necessary for these kinds of differentiated assessments. If we wonder why many teachers of at-risk students rely almost exclusively on "worksheets" and "seat work" to assess students' learning, we can understand how this might happen given this information about social skill development. However, just because students might not be "ready" to work with a partner or in a group, does not mean that the teacher should give up on helping to bring those students to a higher level of social performance.

Caution: Students may not show adequate levels of social skill development with one or more teachers, but they may demonstrate these skills with other teachers. Sometimes the only way to tell if a student is truly socially delayed or damaged is if he or she shows social skill deficiency in all classrooms. What may appear to be a student's lack of skills may be a reflection of a teacher's lack of skills.

Bevel and Jordan (2003, p. 87) also include a guideline for determining which kinds of social skills might be necessary to do certain kinds of work as shown in Figure 3.2.

Figure 3.2. Work Guidelines

Task	*Level I*	*Level II*	*Level III*	*Level IV*
Partner work	XXXXXXXX	XXXX		
Small group	XXXXXXXX	XXXXXXXXX	XXXX	
Medium group (more than four participants)	XXXXXXXX	XXXXXXXXX	XXXXXXXXX	XXXX
Able to lead or participate in conflict resolution	XXXXXXXX	XXXXXXXXX	XXXXXXXXX	XXXXXXXXX

How to Assess Students' Social Functioning

The best way to assess students' social functioning is by closely observing them, interviewing them and surveying them to determine how they rate themselves. In addition to having group and individual conversations with students about their social skills, teachers might use a checklist such as Figure 3.3 to give students at the beginning of the year to act as a baseline and a preassessment prior to students' attempting to participate in partner or group activities.

Figure 3.3. Social Skills Assessment

Answer the following questions true or false.

1. I know the names of most of the students in our class and/or I want to learn their names as soon as possible. T F

2. When someone is talking to me, I look at them and watch their faces. T F

3. I respect everyone in the class even if I don't always agree with what they say and do. T F

4. I understand and can always follow the rules of the class. T F

5. I can work in a group with anybody in this class. T F

6. I always clean up after myself. T F

7. If someone in my group is messy, I feel it is my responsibility to clean up after them. T F

8. I have never had a physical fight with another student. T F

9. Everyone in the class, including the teacher, deserves my respect no matter what. T F

10. If I have a problem with someone, I can work it out without disrupting the class. T F

Many students will not answer this assessment honestly; however, the teacher might get a good sense of where the student would like to be if he or she practiced. The teacher might also provide opportunities for peers to evaluate each other, by requiring students to reflect about the behavior of fellow group members. The teacher should evaluate regularly and update assessments at least quarterly. Figure 3.4 is a checklist teachers might use to evaluate students' social skills.

Figure 3.4. Social Skills Assessment Form

Rate each student on the grid below as having ability levels on four important social skills. Give each student a 1–4 for each of these four skills.

1 = no skill; 2= some skills; 3 = abilities within normal limits; 4 = exceptional ability

Skill 1: Student is respectful of peers and authority and can empathize with others.

Skill 2: Student understands how to stay with a group and stay seated until the teacher prompts him or her to move (lacks impulsivity).

Skill 3: Student solves problems effectively without fighting or disrupting class (lacks impulsivity).

Skill 4: Student takes appropriate responsibility for doing what is right.

Name	Skill 1	Skill 2	Skill 3	Skill 4	Overall Level/ Comments

What is critical here is that teachers realize that so much depends on their own ability to establish a caring relationship based on reasonable expectations and consistency and that they must *teach* at-risk students social skills. *Teachers should not assume that socially challenged students will never be able to work successfully in groups.*

Assessing At-Risk Students' Attitudes about Success

Key Factors

Assessment of students' experiences and interpretations of a school's (often hidden) curriculum is critical if teachers want to successfully address the needs of at-risk students. These marginalized students experience a lack of belonging in the school and in the world of academic achievement; therefore, to assess their learning, teachers need to also assess their attitudes about and interest in each unit of study. Understanding students' interests and designing assessments that match them help at-risk students internalize rather than externalize the curriculum and the results of learning (Sagor & Cox, 2004).

It is important for teachers to understand how students *attribute* their success. According to Alderman (1990) there are four different ways:

1. Internal/stable—achievement (poor or excellent) comes from inside the student and is consistent (the achiever vs. the loser).

2. Internal/unstable—achievement (poor or excellent) comes from inside the student and is not consistent. Student attributes achievement to how much work he or she does.

3. External/stable—achievement (poor or excellent) comes from factors outside the student's control and is consistent. Student feels powerless to have any effect on success or failure. Lucky or unlucky.

4. External/unstable—achievement (poor or excellent) that comes from factors outside the student's control is inconsistent. Student feels that others control his or her success or failure. He or she may attribute success based on how much help the teacher or friend supplies.

See Sagor and Cox (2004) for an extended discussion. Many at-risk students attribute their success to external sources. *Teachers should attempt to use differentiated assessment to help at-risk students develop an internal locus of control of their success.*

Effects of the Teachers' Classroom Management Capabilities and Style on Assessment of At-Risk Students

If teachers do not have the attention and respect of at-risk students in the classroom, they cannot teach them, much less assess their learning. It is a priority, therefore, that teachers pay close attention to the *academic needs* of at-risk students as they affect their management of the classroom. According to Jones and Jones (1990), as cited in Sagor and Cox (2004), at-risk students have the following academic needs:

♦ Understanding the teachers' goals

♦ Being involved in the learning process

♦ Relating to the content of the instruction

♦ Being able to follow their own interests

♦ Receiving immediate and realistic feedback

♦ Experiencing success

♦ Experiencing appropriate structure

♦ Having time to integrate learning activities

♦ Having positive contact with peers

♦ Having instruction that matches their cognitive development and learning styles

Teachers can develop an assessment tool of their own based on this information or they can use the one from Sagor and Cox (p. 180) to assess the academic needs of at-risk students. If teachers cannot meet these needs, they will most likely experience behavior problems from these students.

Teacher Voices on Using Assessment to Build Relationships with At-Risk Students

Waldo Rogers, who typically has an excellent relationship with students at Lowe's Grove Middle School, says that you cannot teach at-risk students until they like you and trust you. He exemplifies the old saw, "Students don't care what you know until they know that you care." Teachers may use the assessment process to show at-risk students that they care and that they will help them learn.

Don Dixon, who has excellent rapport with *all* of his students, says he builds a "triangle" with his students. The triangle works like this: The teacher loves his subject, the students love the teacher, so the students show that they love the subject the teacher is teaching them by doing well on assessments. After 30 years of teaching, Don Dixon says this triangle has rarely failed him.

Dixon also uses a special classroom management technique based on his belief that the teacher should create the correct atmosphere for learning by creating "high and low points in the lesson." He uses a method he calls "Heads Down, Eyes Closed" at strategic points during the lesson. For example, when he senses that students are becoming too loud and chaotic, he will call, "heads down, eyes closed." All students comply with his request, and he is able to redirect them toward more controlled behavior. He also uses this technique if he wants to make sure students are listening carefully to a very short directive. He does not use this method for longer directives because he realizes most of his students need visual as well as auditory cues to attend to and remember what he is asking them to do.

Another idea that will "get at-risk students" on the teacher's side occurs when the teacher has a "desk conference" with the student and discovers that he or she has a good answer to one of the assessment questions. The teacher can call on that student to answer that specific question during class discussion. Helping the at-risk student "look good" goes a long way toward building good relationships with these students through the assessment process.

Planning Effective Assessments for At-Risk Students

When teachers design assessments for at-risk students, they need to keep the following ideas in mind:

- For any assessment, the teacher needs to make sure to start with questions students can answer without the teacher's help. In other words, the teacher needs to plan assessments that students can begin independently. If the teacher starts with difficult ideas or processes, at- risk students may become frustrated and as a result may act out and disrupt everyone.

- Teachers should not expect "busy work" to satisfy the needs of at-risk students. They recognize when teachers are giving them work that is too easy.

- Poorly managed cooperative learning assessments can create problems for at-risk students and can result in what Sagor and Cox (2004) call "sanctioned abandonment" by the teacher. As mentioned earlier in this chapter, some of these students may not be socially "ready" for cooperative learning activities. In addition to being socially inept, at-risk students may not do well in some forms of cooperative learning because they tend to leave the work to academically stronger students. The result is that they feel even more left out and inadequate.

- A quality service learning project can provide excellent differentiated assessment potential for at-risk students because feeling needed facilitates self-esteem and belonging.

In summary, at-risk students need to see the relevance of assessments. If they cannot see a clear relationship between the assessment and their real world, they will not take the assignment seriously and will not be motivated to achieve. In other words, for at-risk students, teachers should base assessments on authentic standards that have value in the real world. If the teachers of at-risk students want to have the best chance for success on assessments, it is critical that they make the following clear:

- Learning objectives, targets, goals

- Expected performance or product

- Criteria for evaluation (Sagor & Cox, 2004)

Examples of Preassessments: Feelings and Beliefs about Topic

Figure 3.5 is a short survey to use for math.

Figure 3.5. Math Interest Survey

Are You a Mathematician?

Please answer the following questions as thoroughly as you can.

1. What strategies do you use when you do math?

2. How would you describe your math abilities? (You can use a scale of 1–10 with 10 being highest and 1 being lowest.)

3. What roles does math serve in people's personal and public lives?

4. What roles will math play in your future education and career goals?

5. List three goals you plan to work toward to help you develop as mathematician.

Survey adapted from *I read it, but I don't get it: Comprehension strategies for adolescent readers,* by C. Tovani, 2000, Portland, Me: Stenhouse Publishers; and *Reading for understanding: A guide to improving reading in middle and high school classrooms: The reading apprenticeship guidebook,* by R. Schoenbach, C. Greenleaf, C. Cziko, & L. Hurwitz, 1999, San Francisco, CA: Jossey-Bass.

Science teachers can easily adapt this short survey and rename it "Are You a Scientist?"

Procedures

Step 1: Make sure students have a pencil or pen.

Step 2: Hand out the survey to the whole class.

Step 3: Either as a whole class, if all students are at-risk, or to certain clustered students or individuals, have students read the first question aloud and explain what they mean with examples.

Step 4: Ask students to write their response to the first question and allow enough time by observing when most have finished writing. Do not wait for all the students to finish writing if there are extremely slow responders. Keep the pace in line with the majority of the class or trouble might arise from bored students. The slower ones will catch up when sharing time comes.

Step 5: Ask volunteers to share their responses and also use demand response.

Continue this process until the class has answered all questions.

Examples of Preassessments: Content

Figures 3.6 is a science example of an Anticipation Guide. Teachers should write the statements in terms that do not over-challenge at-risk students.

Procedures

Step 1: Hand out the Anticipation Guide and ask students to find the answers in a text.

Step 2: Students may complete the process individually, with a partner, or in a small group.

Step 3: After the students have responded to the guide, make a list with the whole class showing how many students agreed or disagreed with the statement.

Step 4: Students read the text to correct their answers.

Step 5: Conduct another whole class discussion about the correct answers.

Figure 3.6. Matter: Anticipation Guide 1

Read the statements below and decide if you agree (A) or disagree (D) with each statement. Write your answer in the left column under Anticipation. After you have learned about the topic, complete the right column under Reaction. Notice what you have learned.

Anticipation	Statement	Reaction
	1. A mixture includes lots of different things.	
	2. All matter is made of only four elements: air, earth, fire, and water.	
	3. When you see a rusty car, you are observing a chemical reaction.	
	4. When you bake a cake, you are mixing homogeneous substances.	
	5. If you leave salt water in a dish, the water will evaporate, and the salt will be left in the dish.	
	6. If you spilled your M & M's into a bowl of metal shavings, the best way to clean them is with a magnet.	

Anticipation	Statement	Reaction
	7. All things are made of the most basic particle, the molecule.	
	8. When water boils, it changes to a gas.	
	9. When water freezes, we are observing a physical property.	
	10. When wood burns, we are observing a physical property.	

Key: 1. A; 2. D; 3. A; 4. D; 5. A; 6. A; 7. D; 8. A; 9. A; D. 10. D

Note: Leveled versions of this same Anticipation Guide appear in Chapters 4 and 5.

Interview Using Accountable Talk

Procedures

According to Fisher & Frey (2007), at-risk students often lack the skills to participate in academically oriented conversations; therefore, the teacher might use accountable talk, which is a framework for teaching students how to talk to one another about an academic topic. This process was developed in 2000 by Lauren Resnick and a team of researchers (Fisher & Frey, 2007). In accountable talk, at-risk students make a commitment to do the following:

- Stay on the assigned topic.

- Talk about information that is accurate and relevant to the topic.

- Listen to partners and think about what they are saying.

Prior to allowing students to interview one another, the teacher should make sure that they understand accountable talk and are committed to using it. To structure the interview, the teacher should give students an interview template (Figure 3.7) and ask them to find out what at least three other students in the class already know about the topic. They might then turn the template in so that the teacher may get a better idea about what students already know. Students can also take turns sharing what they found out in their interviews. What follows is a useful template for the interviews.

Figure 3.7. Interview Template

Topic: _____ Your name: _____

Student 1: _____ (name) What he or she thinks about the

topic:_____

_____

_____

_____

_____

_____

_____

_____

_____

_____

_____

_____

Student 2:_____ (name) What he or she thinks about the
topic:_____

_____

_____

_____

_____

_____

_____

Student 3:_____ (name) What he or she thinks about the
topic_____

_____

_____

_____

_____

_____

_____

_____

_____

_____

_____

_____

Informal Assessment

Musical Chairs Example

Processes

Latekka Lewis uses an adapted musical chairs activity as a way of reviewing concepts through a kinesthetic, brain-based method. She follows this process:

1. She picks her music and her questions for students to answer. The questions need to have one right answer so that there is no debate.

2. She does not alter her classroom too much to do this. She merely tells her students to walk around the classroom, and when the music stops, they must find a chair. Of course she has removed enough chairs so that one student is always left standing.

3. The student left standing each time must answer the question.

Formative Assessments

Formative assessments allow teachers to determine if their students are learning what the teacher is teaching them. It is assessment *for* learning (Stiggins, et al., 2006), not *of* learning. What follows are several examples of differentiated formative assessment strategies that will help the teacher scaffold assessment for at-risk students.

Differentiating Assessment: Six Part Template

Template Parts Two through Five

For each formative assessment example, teachers will see how to address Parts Two through Five of the Differentiating Assessment Template. The first part of this chapter covered Part One for *all* examples. Teachers can only complete Part Six after they have implemented the assessment. What follows is a review of the template:

Figure 3.8. Differentiating Assessment: Six-Part Template

Students' Needs (described in detail at the beginning of this chapter)				
2. Curriculum				
Standard Course of Study (SCOS)	**Essential Question (EQ)**	**K**now	**U**nderstand	**D**o *(See MO below)*
3. Measurable Objective (MO)				
Introduction	Thinking verb(s)	Product	Response Criterion	Content
4. Differentiation				
Readiness		Interests		Learning Styles
5. Assessment Procedures (listed as steps)				
6. Assessment Audit (to be completed at the end of the assessment)				

Differentiated Formative Assessments by Learning Styles

For the assessment strategies that follow, the work of Silver, Strong, and Perini (2007) provides the differentiated assessment categories, which include the following: Mastery, understanding, self-expression, interpersonal, and four-style. I have adapted many of the strategies explained in Silver et al. (including using alternative names for some similar concepts), and I have focused on structuring the aspect of their usefulness as math and science assessment strategies for at-risk students.

Mastery-Based Formative Assessment

Direct Instruction Example

This mastery strategy allows for constant formative assessment during guided practice and independent practice (updated Madeline Hunter by Robin Hunter, 2004; Marzano, et al., 2001; Figure 3.9).

Figure 3.9. Direct Instruction

Curriculum				
SCOS	**EQ:** How might we use two-step equations to solve real world problems?	**K**now—how to solve two-step equations	**U**nderstand that two-step equations are useful to solve real world problems	**D**o—solve increasingly difficult two-step equations *(See MO below)*

Measurable Objective				
Introduction	**Thinking Verbs**	**Product**	**Response Criterion**	**Content**
Students will…	interpret and execute	showing work and providing answers	that are correct	using two-step equations to solve problems.

Differentiation		
Readiness—teacher uses grouping based on mastery	**Interests**—grouping based on mastery decreases students' boredom	**Style**—mathematical/ logical, mastery, analytical

Procedures

For at-risk students, it is important to provide as much direct and guided practice as necessary to assure their learning. This includes giving these students more chances to practice, to receive teacher feedback, and to revise their work. With at-risk students, it is a good idea for teachers to ask students to help them decide when to move on to each level of practice as shown in Figure 3.10.

Figure 3.10. Math Example of Direct Instruction Assessment

Modeling

The teacher can model a lesson, such as solving a two-step equation using the following teaching methods:

♦ Visual—writing an example of a two-step equation on a board or overhead

♦ Oral—explaining orally how to solve that two-step equation

♦ Kinesthetic—asking students to write the two-step equation on a sheet of paper or having them role-play the process using their fingers, bodies, or manipulatives

Assessment

♦ Direct practice: Work as many two-step equation problems as the students appear to need. Ask students directly if they have had enough modeling. Take a vote with thumbs up or down to determine if the majority of the class is ready for assessment. Do not belabor the point to the degree that too many students are bored.

Guided practice: Give students 10 two-step equations to solve on their own. Collect the work to determine if students have complete, partial, or no mastery of the process. Divide students into three groups as follows:

Group 1:

Mastery group solves enrichment word problems that require them to use their ability to apply two-step equations to solve the problems in an enrichment project. Students may collaborate to solve the problems, but each student completes the work. Here is an example of a real-world problem that requires two-step equations and that at-risk students may be able to solve.

Problem: You are planning a school fund raiser, and you want to buy bags of candy for students to sell. You have $256 to spend. Each bag of candy costs $1.50, and shipping is $2.00. How many bags of candy can you order?

You want to make a 30% profit. How much should you charge for each bag of candy students sell?

How much money will you make?

Make a poster advertising the candy (optional).

Group 2:

Partial mastery group solves more simple two-step equations within small groups. Teachers troubleshoot with this group but ask them to do their best to help each other complete the problems.

Individual practice: The teacher retests individually with five sample two-step equation problems and then moves students on to enrichment or to a reteaching group.

Group 3: No mastery group requires reteaching two-step equations using colored blocks or other manipulatives. Students practice solving several simple problems with teacher's help.

    Individual practice: The teacher retests individuals with five easy two-step equation problems, and then moves on to enrichment or to reteaching group.

♦ On the next day, the teacher allows the enrichment group to complete their work and then helps the students who advanced to enrichment. The students who make up the second wave of enrichment work will most likely need more one-on-one help than did the first group. The teacher should evaluate the work of the first enrichment group so that they might feel confident about their answers and their ability to solve the enrichment problem.

♦ For the group that is still having problems, the teacher should provide more practice with manipulatives and explanation. If those students still do not learn the process of solving two-step equations in three direct instruction lessons, the teacher needs to find out-of-class ways to help those students master the topic.

    Note: Teachers should not assume that just because the students have mastered the process of solving two-step equations that they will continue to show mastery of this skill. Revisit this skill on each unit test for the remainder of the year. Teachers should use a spiraling assessment pattern where *no skill is left behind*, and the teacher does not assume that the skill is located in long-term memory.

Understanding-Based Formative Assessment

Using graphic organizers to show how various concepts and ideas are similar and different can help at-risk students improve their higher-order thinking ability (Marzano, et al., 2001; Figure 3.11).

Figure 3.11. Compare and Contrast Example

Curriculum				
SCOS	**EQ:** What are the differences between bacteria and viruses?	**K**now—similarities and differences between bacteria and viruses	**U**nderstand that knowing the similarities and differences between bacteria and viruses helps us better solve problems related to them	**D**o—determine similarities and differences between bacteria and viruses *(See MO below)*

Measurable Objective				
Introduction	**Thinking Verbs**	**Product**	**Response Criterion**	**Content**
Students will…	generate, and compare	using a Venn diagram	to include at least three differences and three similarities	between bacteria and viruses.

Differentiation		
Readiness—graphic organizer provided by the teacher scaffolds assessment	**Interests**—students note ideas that interest them	**Style**—understanding, visual, investigative

Procedures

The strategy includes four phases for students: (1) observe or read, (2) compare using a graphic organizer, (3) draw conclusions about comparisons, and (4) summarize learning about comparisons. Teacher can note achievement at phases 2 through 4.

To scaffold this assignment, teachers should include a text that students can read independently (the Internet is a good resource), or if that kind of text cannot be found, use a shared reading strategy that allows all students access to the text. Show students how to fill out at least one line in Similarities and one in Differences. Notice that for at-risk students, the teacher should supply the middle boxes concerning how to categorize the differences between bacteria and virus (Figure 3.12).

**Figure 3.12. Similarities and Differences Graphic Organizer—
Science Example**

As you read the chapters, complete this organizer.
What is being compared and contrasted?

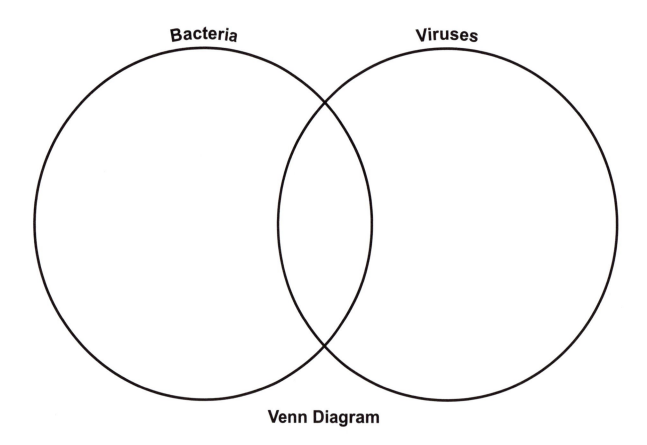

Venn Diagram

Self-Expression–Based Formative Assessment

Inductive Learning Example

This is a brainstorming and predicting process that includes grouping, labeling and generalizing to construct essential ideas. It is a wonderful assessment strategy to use if teachers want students to practice using inductive reasoning (Taba, 1971; Silver, Strong, & Perini, 2007).

Figure 3.13. Inductive Learning Example

Curriculum				
SCOS	**EQ:** How are electricity and magnets related	**K**now—how to construct generalizations about magnets and electricity through an inductive process	**U**nderstand—see listed possible generalizations on page 85	**D**o—visit learning centers to experience various aspects of magnets and electricity, generalize from these experiences *(See MO below)*

Measurable Objective				
Introduction	**Thinking Verbs**	**Product**	**Response Criterion**	**Content**
Students will…	compare, explain, generate, attribute, implement, and check	by recording in writing	correct answers to questions from each of six learning stations	about magnetism and electricity.

Differentiation		
Readiness—teacher-led process and experiential learning activities scaffold assessment	**Interests**—movement through a variety of learning experiences encourages interest for most students	**Style**—self-expression, visual, investigative, kinesthetic

Procedures

At-risk students can truly enjoy this process because it does not have to include very much reading and writing, which often deny them access to learning activities. What follows is a science example of an inductive learning assessment strategy (Figure 3.14).

Figure 3.14. Magnetism and Electricity

Set up mini-assessment stations (learning stations) that show various aspects of magnetism and electricity.

Note: For at-risk students the number of mini-assessment stations should allow no more than four students to experience the station at one time.

Give each student a booklet or journal that will guide his or her experiences in the mini-stations. (Booklet begins on the next page.)

Magnetism and Electricity Observations Booklet

Magnetism & Electricity Generalizations

By: _____

Date: _____

Magnets Station

Compare and contrast these two types of magnets in the Venn diagram below:

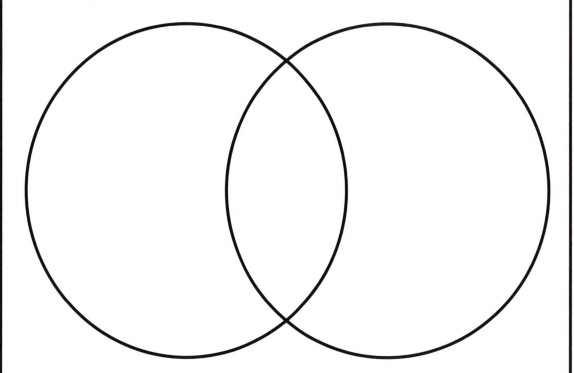

Draw a picture of one thing the magnets will attract and one thing it will not attract. Explain what is happening.

Magnetic Poles

Describe what you notice when you attempt to attach the magnets to each other. Draw a conclusion about what you observe and make a drawing of it in the spaces below: What do you notice?

Describe:_____

Draw a picture of what you observe:

Making Magnets

Magnetize a paper clip by rubbing it with one pole of the magnet. Read the passage about destroying magnets and breaking magnets. Fill out the chart below about these three processes.

What happens when you make a magnet?	How can you destroy a magnet?	What happens when you break a magnet?

Electrical Current and Magnetic Fields

Note which way the needle on the compass is pointing. Take turns putting the compass under the center of the wire. Observe the change in the compass and record your observations.

Observations:

Electromagnetic Art

Using magnets and colored iron filings create patterns. Draw your favorite patterns below and explain how the magnet made this pattern.

How does it work?

Making Electricity

Hold the wire between the two poles of a horseshoe magnet. As you move the wire up and down, notice what happens to the meter. Draw a picture of the meter before and after you use the wire. Explain why this happens.

Before	After

Explain why this happens:

Page 6

Generalizations

Write at least two generalizations based on your observations in the learning stations.

Generalization 1

Generalization 2

Page 7

Setting Up Mini-Stations

1. Magnets station: Have two types of magnets in a box with various things that the magnets will attract and some things the magnet will not attract. Ask students to record their observations on the appropriate page in their Magnetism and Electricity journal. This mini-station will assess students' abilities to compare and contrast the types of magnets and to note things that will and will not respond to magnetic pull.

2. Magnetic poles: In a box have two bar magnets with labeled north and south poles. Ask students to describe what they notice when they attempt to attach the magnets to each other and ask them to draw a conclusion about what they observe and to make a drawing of it.

3. Making magnets: In a box or on a platter, have some paper clips and a strong magnet. Directions instruct students to magnetize a paper clip by rubbing it with one pole of the magnet. Have a short passage from which students may read about destroying magnets and breaking magnets. They make a chart about these three processes.

4. Electrical current and magnetic fields: On a tray have a D battery attached to safe wires that connect to a small light bulb. Put a small compass on the tray and have instructions that tell students to note which way the needle on the compass is pointing. The instructions should tell students to take turns putting the compass under the center of the wire. Students observe the change in the compass and record their observations.

5. Electromagnetic art: Using magnets and colored iron filings, students create patterns. They draw their favorite patterns.

6. Making electricity: On a tray, place a sensitive multimeter that is connected to a 1-meter wire. The instructions tell students to hold the wire between the two poles of a horseshoe magnet. As students move the wire up and down, they notice what happens to the meter.

7. Students write at lease two generalizations based on their observations. Some generalizations might be as follows:

   Magnets attract some things but not others.

   Magnets have two poles that attract each other if the poles are opposite each other but repulse each other if they are the same.

   A person can make a magnet by rubbing a piece of metal on an existing magnet.

   Magnetic fields interfere with the functioning of a compass.

   Magnetism can create electricity.

The assessment should proceed as follows:

1. Introduce the topic of magnets and electricity and the concept of generalizing. Tell students that they will be "discovering" some possibly new ideas about magnets and electricity so that they might "generalize." Explain "generalizing" as drawing conclusions or making statements about findings. Give an example such as the following: A person smiles when you walk by, they laugh at your jokes, they say nice things to you when you talk, and they "have your back." What might you generalize about that person from this information? Answers should be something similar to: He or she is a friend. *Note:* It is a good idea to make sure at-risk students understand what you want them to do, and it is a good idea to use examples that are meaningful to them.

2. Explain the process. Tell students that they will rotate through six learning centers to make observations and record information. Give each student a copy of their assignment booklet titled, Magnetism and Electricity Generalizations, and tell them they will be assigned to a group. Explain that their group will move to each center every few minutes (the number of minutes depends on how many stations are planned, how much time will be spent at each station, and how much time students need to complete each observation.)

3. Assign groups. This process flows most smoothly if group assignments are already written out so that they may be displayed.

4. Start the process. Give a signal such as a bell, flicking lights, or other signal that has been rehearsed with the students.

5. After everyone has visited each learning station, reconvene a whole-class session to complete the generalizations. Give students another example of a possible generalization and then ask them to write two of their own.

6. Students turn in their work. Assess their learning about the topic. Having this kind of information will help plan future instruction and assessments of this topic.

Metaphorical Expression or Synectics Example

This is a way of assessing students' ability to make meaning through a creative process of comparison. This type of assessment may seem to be a stretch for at-risk students; however, with some teacher structuring, these students can enjoy the creativity this process allows (Gordon, 1961; Silver, Strong, Perini, 2007).

Figure 3.15. Synectics Assessment

Curriculum				
SCOS	**EQ:** How is geometry like a dance? How is a dance like geometry?	**K**now—how to use synectics to better understand geometry	**U**nderstand that geometry is like a dance, and a dance is like geometry	**D**o—use synectics to discover how geometry is like dance *(See MO below)*

Measurable Objective				
Introduction	**Thinking Verbs**	**Product**	**Response Criterion**	**Content**
Students will...	generate, compare, create, and critique	metaphorical statements and creative products	that expand and enhance	understanding of geometry and dancing.

Differentiation		
Readiness—teacher-led process, art, and acting out concepts to make them more concrete	**Interests**—students inspired to be creative	**Style**—self-expression, visual, investigative, kinesthetic, artistic, aesthetic

Procedures

Using whole-class interaction and art can make this higher-level thinking process accessible to at-risk students. Figure 3.16 is a math example of the synectics process.

In each step, the teacher or designated student records the remarks of students as they brainstorm. The teacher makes it clear to students that no answer is silly or stupid, and no one should criticize or make negative comments about any remark.

Figure 3.16. Synectics—Geometry

Step 1: Topic: What is geometry? Record all answers students might give about the meaning of geometry. Answers could be as follows: It is a type of math; it is about shapes; it takes abstract thinking; it is about finding perimeters and areas; it is about angles; it solves unknowns, has patterns; it helps us build buildings; it helps us do better art if we know how to scale; it is about measurement.

Step 2: Create an analogy: How is geometry like dancing? Both have parts, both have unknowns, both have abstract ideas, both have patterns, both have shape, both have or make lines, both can be performed, both can be drawn, both have balls. The teacher asks students to visualize and feel how a dance might be like geometry. A round dance, square dance, dance with angles, dance with area, dance with patterns, shapes that can be danced, angles that make a dance.

Step 3: The teacher asks students to draw one of the analogies on a sheet of paper. For example a dancing angle, a round or square dance, a dancing shape. Instead of drawing, or in addition to drawing, ask students to come to the front of the class and act out one of the analogies.

Step 4: Students explore as a whole-class discussion or with a partner how some of the words they have listed seem to be in conflict.
Examples: "Performing" and "drawing" seem to conflict because one is with the full body, and the other is just with the hand. Drawing seems to be one-dimensional and performing seems two-dimensional.
"Round dance" and "square dance" seem to conflict because one is angular and pointed, and the other is circular and smooth.
"Ball" and "line" seem to conflict because line is one-dimensional, and ball is two-dimensional. Ball has area, and line only has surface. Ball can bounce, and line rests on the page without movement.

Step 5: Create a new analogy. Students propose new analogies and vote on a new one based on their drawings and performances. For example, students could decide that the best new analogy compares sharp to smooth or line to ball.

Step 6: Look for words or phrases that "redefine" geometry, that make it more meaningful and a richer experience. For example, when we dance we can think about how geometry provides shape and form to our movements. When we do geometry we can see how the shapes and lines dance. Here are some suggestions for assessment products:

♦ A group or individual dance performance that demonstrates an understanding of the angles that form geometrical shapes.

♦ A story board or comic book about shapes that dance.

♦ A report on how popular dance reflects shapes and forms.

♦ A picture that incorporates a certain number of geometrical shapes.

Interpersonal-Based Assessment

Reciprocal Learning Example

Interpersonal-based assessments use students' natural inclination to help each other and work together; however, with at-risk students, these kinds of activities can be tricky if teachers do not feel that students are ready for them. If teachers are closely monitoring the students' social skill level, they may conclude that most, but not all of the students can participate in these kinds of assessments. If some students cannot be successful working with others, teachers should consider assigning them to do the work on their own.

Figure 3.17. Reciprocal Learning Example

Note: This process can be highly successful with at-risk students if they are adequately prepared. This example is adapted from the work of Silver, Strong, and Perini, 2007.

Curriculum				
SCOS	**EQ:** How might students work together to solve multistep algebraic equations?	**K**now—how to coach someone through the process of solving multistep algebraic equations	**U**nderstand that students can help each other through solving multistep algebraic equations	**D**o—coach a peer through solving several multistep algebraic equations *(See MO below)*

Measurable Objective				
Introduction	**Thinking Verbs**	**Product**	**Response Criterion**	**Content**
Students will…	explain, execute, and check	another students' work	to make sure the student accurately solves	multistep algebraic equations.

Differentiation		
Readiness—teacher-led process, with structured practice, individualizing for those not ready	**Interests**—working together is interesting to most students	**Style**—interpersonal, mathematical, logical, analytical, auditory

Procedures

Before actually using the process to work through an assignment, the teacher might use some warm-up or practice sessions to test students' readiness to tackle the real strategy.

Practice Sessions for Math or Science

Step 1: Tell students that they are going to practice a process called "reciprocal teaching." Tell them that they need to carefully select a partner who will work with them for several sessions. Do not allow three students to work together. If the students create a problem about this, suggest that they may not be "ready" to practice this skill. If any student seems uninterested in working with a partner, or indicates they will create problems, have an individualized assignment ready to give them (you should already have a good idea which students will need alternative assignments). Have a place set aside for that student or those students to work. This could include having an arrangement with the media center staff or with another teacher for quiet space. Hopefully most students will be interested and will try this strategy.

Step 2: Tell students that they should next decide who is partner A and who is B. Encourage students to write this information down so that they can remember it for the future. Allow students to pin labels on themselves if that will help them remember their roles.

Step 3: Give the partners an easy task. For example, ask A to find out five facts about B in 2 minutes. Require A to listen to B and to record his or her facts. Stop the process at 2 minutes, and then ask A to report what he or she found out about B. Repeat the process with B finding five facts about A in 2 minutes.

Step 4: Give partners a somewhat more complicated task. Ask A to interview B to find out B's most difficult subject in school and to explain why it is the hardest. A should record B's answers. After B has made sure he or she understands A's ideas, then B should respond by relating his or her own experiences with the subject A has found difficult. A should record what B says. Allow about 5 minutes for this discussion. Next B reports on this discussion, and then they repeat the process with B saying his or her most difficult subject and A responding. If too many of the partners have the same difficult subject, pick another topic, such as, name your least favorite day of the week and why. Focus on problems so that students begin to help each other solve problems.

Math Example Following Practicing

Step 5: If student partners completed the practicing process successfully, tell them they are ready to learn how to "coach" each other. Tell them that coaching is about helping each other do school work, and ask one of your best students to come up to the front of the class to model the process of coaching. Choose a math problem about which students have just started learning and ask the student to work the problem. Describe what the student is doing at each step. For example: Use a multistep equation such as $2x + x + 12 = 66$.

Listen as the student explains the steps he or she should take. Agree either that the student is doing the problem correctly or ask if the student needs to do something else. Realizing that "the blind could be leading the blind," suggest to coaches that they might call the teacher over, or help the student consult the textbook to make sure they are proceeding in the right direction. Show that the role of the coach is to make sure the student is doing the problems correctly and that he or she might use resources if he or she is not sure that his or her help is correct. This process assures that both the coach and the coached are practicing the skill and makes it more likely that students will be motivated to work if the process is interpersonal.

Step 6: Present the partners with a multistep math assignment from the textbook, workbook, or teacher-made list (which is best) for A and ask B to coach him or her through the completion of it. After A has finished the assignment and turned it in, then give B an assignment which A helps him or her complete. Make sure the problems are similar and not too difficult at the beginning of this process.

Grade students' work as coaches separately, but give them both similar grades if they are proceeding correctly. Make sure to be available constantly for support especially at the beginning and especially with new skills.

An adaptation of this process can occur at the end of the year or at the end of a unit. Divide the board in half or use two boards. Write on one side: "I need help with these math skills," and on the other "I can coach someone on how to use these math skills."

Make a list of major math skills and leave space for names on both sides. The major concepts students need to understand for a summative assessment, for example, are as follows: solving equations, solving inequalities, ratios and proportions, graphs and functions, and multiplying fractions. In other words, use fairly large, but discrete topics which depend on whether the this procedure is being used for a unit review or end of year review. Allow one row of students to come to the boards one or two at a time to put their names beside one skill (or more if time permits) on either or both sides. Look at the way students have responded to help pair them appropriately. This strategy works very well if the class is capable of participating in reciprocal teaching.

Four-Style Assessment

Seminar Example

This is a method of assessing students orally. It can be ineffective and counterproductive for at-risk students because most of them are eager to share their thoughts and feelings, but they can become abusive with one another, and they can take a discussion completely out of an academic realm. This is not to say that students should not have opportunities to share their feelings, thoughts, and values, such as in classroom meetings; however, for assessment purpose this kind of assessment is best "tied to a text."

Figure 3.18. Differentiating Assessment—Oral

Curriculum				
SCOS	**EQ:** What do laboratory safety methods teach us about responsibility and cooperation?	**K**now—how to successfully discuss laboratory safety in a seminar session, how to follow the rules of seminar, how to make and support claims	**U**nderstand that laboratory safety teaches us many important concepts such as responsibility and cooperation	**D**o—read a selection, annotate it, write level 2 and 3 questions, follow seminar rules, explore labora-tory safety *(See MO below)*

Measurable Objective				
Introduction	**Thinking Verbs**	**Product**	**Response Criterion**	**Content**
Students will…	explain, summarize, produce, exemplify, attribute, and generate	oral responses	that are respectful of others, thorough, accurate, and reference the text	about laboratory safety.

Differentiation		
Readiness—teacher-led process and practice scaffolds assessments	**Interests**—students think of their own questions and answers in a highly interesting topic	**Style**—interpersonal, mastery, understanding, and self-expression, verbal and linguistic, auditory

Procedures

For at-risk students, it is important to start slowly and increase the time in circles as students improve their skills. Figure 3.19 is an example of a seminar experience for at-risk students, starting with a process useful to both math and science and finishing with a science example.

Figure 3.19. Seminar Assessment—General and Science Example

Step 1: Identify a relatively simple text for the students' first experience with seminar discussion. This text should be broken up with graphics or pictures and should have short paragraphs. Ask students to read this selection and annotate it as best they can (meaning making notes on the side with questions and other ideas). For extremely low-performing students, choose to read and annotate the selection as a whole-class activity.

Step 2: Tell students that during the next class, they will be participating in a seminar discussion of this text and that everyone should bring at least two questions to help with the discussion. At-risk students like to feel that they have some control and input into what happens in class; therefore, allowing them to write questions is motivational. Teach students to write level 2 and 3 type questions. Explain that a level 1 question has one answer, so that it would not be an appropriate discussion question, and then model for them how to construct a level 2 question (one that the person answering must infer and that may have many answers) based on the text they have just read. Walk around the room and have mini desk conferences to make sure each student knows how to write this kind of question. Next teach them how to write a level 3 question, which uses the text as a base but moves beyond it into themes. For at-risk students, provide this stem to get them started on this question level: "What does this text (specify the title of the selection) teach us about…? (Model for them how they might supply a theme idea such as justice, responsibility, violence, etc.) Example: What do laboratory safety methods teach us about responsibility? Check that each student has successfully written a level 3 question. Tell students that their "ticket to seminar is two discussion questions about the text." Make sure each student has written these questions before they leave class, collect them so that they will be available for the next class.

Step 3: For the next class, arrange the desks in a circle. Some teachers might be terrified of moving their desks out of rows, especially for at-risk students, because teachers lose some control when they do not have all eyes facing forward and centered on them. Teachers may want to gradually move into circles by first arranging desks in the following fashion:

Assigning seats ahead of time is the best practice to ward off side conversations between friends. The best way to assign seats is to have a picture of the circle posted with a reference point (a desk, window, or door) to show where the circle starts.

Step 4: At-risk students who may not have experienced a discussion group in a circle may be somewhat agitated; therefore, the teacher should allow some settle-down time and should provide some friendly assurance that students are going to enjoy this activity.

Step 5: As a member of the circle, explain the rules and expectations that are posted in the room, hold them for students to see, or hand out a copy of the rules and expectations to students in addition to posting them. The best rules and expectations for at-risk students are as follows:

Seminar Rules and Expectations

1. Be respectful of everyone. (Seminar is a great chance for at-risk students to practice this social skill. For those students who cannot or will not be respectful for this process, provide an alternative assignment for them. Make sure students understand that monopolizing the group by feeling it is their job to answer all or most of the questions is a form of disrespect. Address this issue as fairly as possible.)

2. You do not need to raise your hand to speak. (This is important because the discussion should be student-controlled, and if students raise their hands, the teacher stays in control.)

3. Keep your eyes on the person who is speaking. (This is important because students will not know when the speaker has finished, and they may begin speaking. It is also the respectful thing to do.)

4. Group conversations only. (Head off this problem by assigning seats in advance.)

5. Reference the text. (Make sure students understand how to help others see their references by making sure everyone knows how to start with page numbers and then identify the correct paragraph.)

6. Use standard English. (Because this process is an oral assessment, hold students accountable to the same standards of correct English as a written assignment. Many teachers leave this expectation out depending on their beliefs about using standard English at school.)

For each of these rules and expectations, stop and ask students to explain why this rule is important and model what it would look like as it is experienced. **This is critical** to the success of a seminar with at-risk students. As the seminar proceeds, gently remind students to follow the correct procedures. Here are some good phrases to use that are successful with at-risk students:

- "Standard English, please"
- "You don't have to raise your hand, just speak out."
- "Can you reference the text?"
- "Help us find the words you are reading"

Step 6: To finish the seminar, give shy or reluctant students a chance to speak. Give these students a "parting shot" question that is relatively easy to answer. To grade a seminar, use the oral assessment grading grid shown in Chapter 2.

Figure 3.20. Science Example

Step 1: Ask students to read a selection on laboratory safety. Go to http://www3.nsta.org/main/news/pdf/tst0509_24.pdf or Google the topic to find wonderful laboratory safety resources that should meet the needs of specific students.

Step 2: Explain how to write level 2 and 3 questions.

Here are some level 2 question examples for this topic:

- Which one of the laboratory safety rules is the most important concerning potential injury to a student?
- Which one of the laboratory safety rules is most important concerning potential disasters for the entire lab?
- What is the most important safety tool a student can use to protect himself or herself from personal injury?
- Why is it important to have laboratory safety rules?

Here are some level 3 question examples:

- What does laboratory safety teach us about responsibility?
- Why are laboratory safety rules important for scientists?
- How might laboratory safety affect the school community?
- How might laboratory safety affect student relationships?

Follow the general rules and expectations for the remainder of this process.

With all of these assessments, it is important to rotate them so that students may have an opportunity to experience each type of assessment.

Summative Assessments for At-Risk Students

Most textbooks provide summative assessments for teachers to use; however, for at-risk students, *it might be best for teachers to create their own unit tests based on their standard course of study and based on students' needs.* To construct a "fair" summative assessment for at-risk students, the teacher might evaluate his or her assessment based on the checklists in Chapter 2.

Constructing Summative Assessments
for At-Risk Students

True/False Tests

True/false questions are problematic because of guessing, which at-risk students are accustomed to doing. One way to solve that problem is to require students to correct statements they believe are false. Figure 3.21 are true/false examples for math and science.

Figure 3.21. True/False for Math and Science

Math

1.   If you subtract $8 - (-4)$ the answer is 4.

2.   When you solve this equation, $7 + 2(x+2)$, and $x = 1$, the answer is 13.

Key: (1. F; 2. T)

For question 1, students might supply the correct answer, which is 12.

Science

1.   A glacier is a large mass of ice that moves slowly over land.

2.   Glaciers erode through a melting process.

Key: (1. T; 2. F)

For question 2, students might correct the statement by stating that glaciers erode through the processes of plucking and abrasion.

Short Answer

See the following math example of a short-answer problem-solving test (Figure 3.22) that is fair to at-risk students because it is "student-friendly." To make this short answer test more interesting to students, teachers might want to use their names in problems she asks them to solve.

Figure 3.22. Test on Solving Systems Using Substitution

Please solve these word problems using substitution. Place the answer in the space provided and show your work on a separate piece of paper. Make sure to number the problem.

1. Your team is planning to go on a field trip to (supply the name of a favorite place they might go, such as an amusement park). Only 93 students turned in their permission slips. If you can only use one school bus (50 seats), how many cars (4 seats each) would you need to get you to the field trip? Answer:

2. _____ and _____ (use students' names) are on the track team. _____ averages 8 m/s and _____ averages 9 m/s for 100-m races. They are racing, and _____ gives _____ a 0.4 s head start. At 0.4, _____ distance is 0 m. Will _____ over-take _____ before the finish line? Answer:
    Explain your answer:

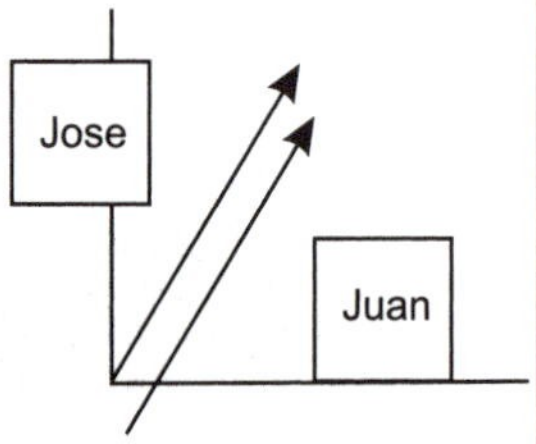

    Jose

    Juan

3. _____ (use students' names) saved $200, and _____ saved $100. At the end of the school year (May), _____ got a part-time job and decided to save $5 per month. _____ decided to add $10 a month to her account from her allowance. How much money will they have in their savings when they have the same amount of money? Answer:

4. _____ (use a student's name) wants to buy a rug for her bedroom, but she is not sure what size the rug should be. The total perimeter of her room is 48 feet. The room is two times wider than it is long. What size rug should _____ buy for her bedroom? Answer:

5. Last year _____ (use a student's name) made a garden in his backyard. He planted only tomatoes and peppers in his 36-foot garden. This year he wants to plant 10 more feet of tomatoes than peppers. How many feet of each crop does he need to plant? Answer:

Multiple Choice

Most textbooks include the capability to construct tests; however, for at-risk students, it is best that teachers construct their own tests. It might even help these students if teachers taught them how to write questions with appropriate distracters. The best kinds of distracters fall into one of these categories: misconception, oversimplification, or overgeneralization. Figure 3.23 is a science example of multiple-choice questions that exemplify each of these types of distracters.

Figure 3.23. Science Example: Analyzing Distracters

1. Which of these statements best describes the function of the cell membrane?
    A. The cell membrane has a breathing function that brings oxygen to the cell (misconception).
    B. The cell membrane helps the cell in many ways (oversimplification).
    C. The cell membrane helps support and protect the cell (overgeneralization).
    D. The cell membrane controls what substances come into and out of the cell (correct answer)

Matching

This is a low-level testing process because the content must be based on facts to be successful.

Crossword Puzzles

To use a crossword puzzle or other word puzzle as a summative assessment with at-risk students, teachers should make sure to do the following:

♦ Provide a list of the words used in the puzzle. At-risk students may not be able to solve the puzzle if they do not know these words.

♦ Although this is a summative assessment, model for students how they might find answers to the puzzle. Some strategies include the following: tell students to look at the chapters from which the words came to find the key terms and names and then determine which definitions written in the text match the definitions or explanations from the puzzle. Also, tell students to read all the definitions first so that they might be looking out for the words they will need for all the spaces.

♦ Without out supplying answers, help highly challenged students get started with the process of finding answers and let students know when they have found correct answers. At-risk students often lack the confidence that they are answering correctly, so that they rely on the teacher to assure them or help them determine if an answer is wrong.

Extended-Writing Response

What follows are some writing prompts for math and science (Figure 3.24). Notice that the prompts are short and to the point because at-risk students may have trouble with longer prompts.

Figure 3.24. Math & Science Writing Prompts
for At-Risk Students

Math Writing Prompts

1. Explain why you love or hate math.

2. If you were in charge of the school, would you make everyone take math? Why or why not?

3. During this course, you have learned about number and operation. Explain in two strong paragraphs (seven or so sentences each), what number and operation mean in the study of mathematics.

4. Explain the law of exponents.

5. Explain how measurement can help teenagers.

6. Why do students need to learn to analyze data? Use examples of types of data that might be useful to students to support your claims.

Science Writing Prompts

1. Think of an important technology (for instance the computer) and explain the effects of that technology on the work of a scientist. You must think of at least three effects.

2. Think of an important health problem experienced by teens and explain how a scientist might help solve it.

3. Explain the effects of erosion on a river.

4. It you were a scientist, which branch of science would you choose, and why?

5. Which branch of science is the most important to you? Why?

For at-risk students, it is important that the teacher help them plan their writing using a graphic organizer. The teacher may actually look at the plan first to determine if students are on the right track before they take time writing. Figure 3.25 is a suggested generic graphic organizer for expository (nonfiction) writing and including persuasion.

Figure 3.25. Writing Organizer

Paragraph 1
Lead (an interesting beginning):
Thesis (reflect the prompt):
Summary of main points:

Paragraph 2
Topic sentence or main idea:
Supporting details (include at least three examples or elaborations):
So what? (includes conclusions you might draw based on your ideas):

Paragraph 3
Topic sentence or main idea:
Supporting details (include at least three examples or elaborations):
So what? (includes conclusions you might draw based on your ideas):

Paragraph 4

Topic sentence or main idea:

Supporting details (include at least three examples or elaborations):

So what? (includes conclusions you might draw based on your ideas):

Paragraph 5

Restated thesis:

Summary of main ideas:

Parting comment (should be a powerful ending):

Projects and Performances

At-risk student do not typically have many opportunities to show what they know through projects.

Project or Performance Assessments

Using Pictures in Math—Performance/Presentation Example

Terrella Davis, Bryant Henderson, and I planned this lesson together based on a common assessment that showed their students were not as a group proficient in solving expressions with unlike terms. The students did not seem to understand that they could not combine 4 with $4y$ or $1y^2$ with $2y$. We decided to combine the classes for the day and ask the students to use pictures to show unlike terms.

Davis and Henderson assigned four to six students per heterogeneous group. They conducted the assessment using these steps:

Step 1: They handed out blocks to remind students how to multiply by grouping the blocks. For example $3 \times 4 = 3$ groups of 4 blocks.

Step 2: They handed out markers, poster paper, and the assessment sheet shown in Figure 3.26.

Figure 3.26. Assessment Sheet

Solving Expressions with Unlike Terms

Name: _____ Date: _____ Period: _____

Group members names: _____

_____

With your group, draw a picture that represents the following:

1. $3(n + 4)$ 2. $2(x + 6)$

3. $4(2y - 1)$ 4. $6(n + n^2)$

5. $2(3x + 2x^2)$ 6. $2(x^2 - 4x + 2)$

7. Explain why your answers to the above expressions are not just one term.

8. Now draw a picture that represents $2(3x + 4x)$. How is the solution to this expression different from the solutions to questions 1–6?

Students presented their group drawings and explanations to the class. Davis and Henderson reassessed students' ability to solve expression with unlike terms and many more, but not all of them, were successful. They offered individual tutoring to those who were unsuccessful.

Protists Art

Science Project Example

Figure 3.27. Science Example of a Project—Protists Art

Protists Art

Protists are creatures that do not have a nucleus in their cells and cannot be classified as animals, plants, or fungi; however, they are *animal-like, plant-like,* and *fungus-like.*

On the pages that follow, draw an example or examples of each type of these diverse creatures. Write a paragraph describing the important features of the category the example represents.

Page 1

Animal-Like Protists

Define:

Draw an example:

Give students blank paper or a space on this assignment page on which to draw their example.

Description:

Page 2

Plant-Like Protists

Define:

Draw an example:

Give students blank paper or a space on this assignment page on which to draw their example.

Description:

Page 3

Fungus-Like Protists

Define:

Draw an example:

Give students blank paper or a space on this assignment page on which to draw their example.

Description:

Page 4

Review:

1. List four types of animal-protists.

    1.

    2.

    3.

    4.

Page 5

Page 5 continues

2. How are these four types of animal-like protists similar to and different from real animals?

   Similarities

   Differences

3. How are plant-like protists similar to and different from real plants?

   Similarities

   Differences

4. In what ways are fungus-like protists similar to and different from real fungi?

   Similarities

   Differences

5. Explain why sunlight is important to plant-like protists.

6. What are the three types of plant-like protists?
   1.
   2.
   3.

7. Would you classify euglena as an animal-like or as a plant-like protest?

   Explain your answer.

Summary

At-risk students require teachers to use special strategies so that they may truly determine what students know and can do before instruction, during instruction, and after it. Teachers could begin by assessing students' social skills and understanding the kinds of assessment that work best with them. The teacher should plan preassessments, informal assessments, formative and summative that capture students' content knowledge and affective experiences.

4

Math and Science Assessments with Moderate to No Scaffolding

Planning assessments for the "regular" or "average" student should be the easiest to do because most resources address the needs of these kinds of students. However, we realize that within this group called "average," we have differing academic strengths, interests, and learning styles; therefore, it is important for the teacher to find out as much as possible about these students keeping in mind cognitive stages of development and psychosocial issues. Even within the realm of the "average" student, we can find great variety in a "regular" (i.e., not special education or gifted) classroom.

This chapter shows teachers specific examples of differentiated assessment strategies that are leveled for students who have average readiness needs. After providing an overview of these students, it provides examples of preassessments, formative assessments, and summative assessments. For the formative assessments, it provides information about using the Differentiating Assessment: Six-Part Template. What follows is a thorough explanation of Part 1 for average students.

Students' Needs—Who Are the Average Students?

Cognitive Development

From ages 6 or 7 years all the way up to 11 or 12 years, which can include some sixth- and seventh-grade students, children are *just beginning* to think logically; they are still in what Piaget calls the "concrete operational stage" of cognitive development (Ginn, 2003). They can reverse a process and see different perspectives; however, they continue to see the future as an extension of the present, and they are still quite concrete. They have not begun to think abstractly. As teachers think about the assessment tasks they plan for 11- or 12-year-old students, they may need to remember that some of them could still be functioning at this level, and this is *normal*. I am highlighting normal because many teachers may consider those students who are still in the concrete operational stage as delayed, and they may feel a need to refer those students to a remedial or learning disabled program. This practice denies the reality of normal development.

If a student is still at the concrete operational stage, teachers cannot expect him or her to predict or infer as well as those students who have moved into a higher stage of cognitive development. Because these students continue to see the future as an extension of the present, they may not be able to abstract a future event or draw a conclusion based on reading between the lines in a text, especially about topics that are foreign to them. These students could also have trouble understanding abstract or even some concrete concepts. Teachers who teach conceptually need to realize that some students may not be able to understand those concepts until they are older. Some theorists, for instance, Hilda Taba (1962) disagree with Piaget's stages. She believes that teachers can move students beyond the confines of a concrete operational stage by conducting a "concept development" process. I have used this process and agree with her to some extent; however, I can still see that some of our average students struggle to think conceptually and inferentially.

From ages 11 or 12 years to adulthood, students can be expected to begin joining the "formal operations stage" of cognitive development. When students are just entering this stage, they may be highly critical because they are still idealistic. This idealism and the tendency to argue with reality characterize many middle school students. Knowing this tendency helps teachers plan assessments that capitalize on this stage of development. Another aspect of this stage that helps teachers with assessment is realizing that some of the younger students (11 or 12 years of age) may not be able to adequately use metacognitive skills. Research has supported the benefits of teachers encouraging students to use metacognitive skills to help them learn more efficiently; however, if a student has not developed that capacity, the teacher could set him or her up for frustration if she does not provide appropriate scaffolding until the student is competent.

As teachers think about "normal" or "average" students, especially those who are 11 or 12 year olds, they need to remember that some of them may struggle with abstract thinking, which includes problems with metacognitive processing, inferring, and thinking conceptually. Teachers need to be prepared to scaffold assessments for these students.

Psychosocial Development

When teachers plan assessments that address the learning needs of the "average" student, they need to understand some of the psychosocial issues with which they are dealing. Teachers need to realize that their students are in the process of developing a sense of identity and that how teachers assess them and give them feedback about their competence or lack of it can help shape that identity (Erikson, 1950). *Attributional theory* (Weiner, 1985) reminds teachers that some students internalize achievement, and others externalize it. If teachers want to be a positive influence in how our 11- to 18-year-old students develop their identities, they need to pay attention to how students view themselves in their abilities to succeed in teachers' assessment of their work. Teachers need to realize the impact they have on the developing identity and be gentle but fair and firm with their assessments. Assessment procedures could damage students' developing identities if teachers do not approach them appropriately.

Math and Science Examples of Preassessments: Feelings and Beliefs about Topic

At the beginning of the year the teacher may want to have some idea about how students view themselves in relationship to math or science.

Procedures

Step 1: Hand out the survey to the whole class.

Step 2: Ask students to read the survey and answer the questions. They might complete it for homework.

Step 3: Go over each question separately and allow plenty of time for all to share.

Step 4: At the end of the discussion, ask students to either verbalize or write a reflection about what they learned about themselves.

Figure 4.1 is a survey the teacher might use at the beginning of the year in a science class. In Chapter 3, there is a similar survey about being a mathematician. The survey is based on ideas from Tovani (2000) and Schoenbach, Greenleaf, Cziko, & Hurwitz, (1999).

Figure 4.1. Beginning of Year Survey

Are You a Scientist?

Please answer the following questions as thoroughly as you can.

1. When you learn about science topics, what helps you remember what you have read or studied?

2. How would you describe your interest in science topics?

3. What roles does science serve in people's personal and public lives?

4. What roles will science play in your future education and career goals?

5. List three goals you plan to work toward to help you develop as science student?

Math and Science Examples of Preassessments: Content

What follows is a science example of an Anticipation Guide for students in the regular educational classroom. There is a similar Anticipation Guide modeled in Chapter 3. Note that this anticipation guide is written at a higher level for average students. Another guide is modeled in Chapter 5 for gifted and highly advanced students.

Procedures

Step 1: Hand out the Anticipation Guide and ask students to find the answers in a text.

Step 2: Students may complete the process individually, with a partner, or in a small group.

Step 3: After the students have responded to the guide, make a list with the whole class showing how many students agreed or disagreed with the statement.

Step 4: Students read the text to correct their answers.

Step 5: Conduct another whole class discussion about the correct answers.

Figure 4.2. Matter: Anticipation Guide 2

Read the statements below and decide if you agree (A) or disagree (D) with each statement. Write your answer in the column under Anticipation. After you have learned about the topic, complete the column under Reaction. Notice what you have learned.

Anticipation	Statement	Reaction
	1. Physical properties are useful to classify matter.	
	2. Every form of matter has both physical and chemical properties.	
	3. Flour is a pure substance.	
	4. A chemical property can be observed without trying to change a substance.	
	5. Classifying substances is easy if we know their physical properties.	
	6. The smallest basic particle is an atom.	
	7. Elements are the simplest substances.	
	8. In a homogeneous mixture you can easily see the different parts.	
	9. A solution is an example of a heterogeneous mixture.	
	10. Compounds are elements that have combined to form properties different from the original elements.	

Key: 1. A ; 2. A; 3. D; 4. D; 5. D; 6. A; 7. A; 8. D; 9. D; 10. A.

3-2-1 Adaptation for Average Students

If teachers are beginning a unit on any math or science topic with average students, they should take into consideration that the students should have *some* prior knowledge that is directly or indirectly associated with the unit of study.

Procedures

Average students may need an example to get them started, but they should be able to write at least three things they know about most math or science topics. For example, if the teacher asks students to list three things they know about "inequalities," they should be able to recall learning about "greater than or less than" symbols in elementary school math. For science, average students may not recall details about how bacteria grow, but they should be able to think of examples of bacteria in their daily lives. They should be able to write two questions and one way they would like to learn about the topic. By asking average students their questions and how they want to learn about a topic, the teacher will be better able to tailor the instruction to meet their needs.

This 3-2-1 assessment is a short and easy way to preassess average students' knowledge, questions, and learning styles regarding a topic in math and science. Teachers may easily use it as a "ticket out the door" assignment. Teachers could hand out cards that look like Figure 4.3.

Figure 4.3. Ticket Out the Door

3-2-1

1. Write **3 things** you already know about decimals.

2. Write **2 questions** you have about decimals.

3. Write **1 way** you would like to learn about this topic.

Informal Assessment

Vocabulary Ball Game—Science

Most average students should be able to handle informal assessments that include playing a game with a ball.

Procedures

Step 1: Ask students to review the unit on Cell Structure and Function in order to identify and define the key terms listed there. Ask them to make flash cards with the term on the front and the definition on the back.

Step 2: Allow time for partners to practice learning the definitions of the terms.

Step 3: Show students how to play a ball game with the science terms. The game goes like this: Throw the ball to a student who catches it. When the student catches the ball, either give him or her a term to define or give him or her the definition, and the student supplies the term.

Step 4: If the student correctly identifies the term or gives the correct definition, then he or she throws the ball to someone else. When that student catches the ball, the student who threw it either gives a term or the definition of a term, and the student who caught the ball must give the correct answer. If the student misses the term, he or she must throw the ball back to the teacher instead of to a classmate.

Another way to do this is to have the teacher ask all the questions, and students throw the ball to each other.

Formative Assessments

Formative assessments allow teachers to determine if their students are learning what the teacher is teaching them. What follows are several examples of differentiated formative assessment strategies that will help the teacher plan assessment for average students.

Differentiating Assessment:
Six-Part Template—Parts 2 to 5

For each assessment example, teachers will see examples of how to address Parts 2 through 5. The first part of the chapter covered Part 1 for all examples, and teachers can only complete Part 6 after they have implemented the assessment. Figure 4.4 is a review of the template for this process:

Figure 4.4. Differentiating Assessment: Six-Part Template

1. Students' Needs–described in detail				
2. Curriculum				
Standard Course of Study (SCOS)	Essential Question (EQ)	Know	Understand	Do *(See MO below)*
3. Measurable Objectives (MOs) The generic template is as follows:				
Introduction	Thinking Verb(s)	Product	Response Criterion	Content
4. Differentiation				
Readiness		Interests		Learning Styles
5. Assessment Procedures—listed by steps				
6. Assessment Audit				

Differentiated Formative Assessments by Learning Styles

For the assessment strategies that follow, I will show how to use differentiated and strategic assessments for average students. I will explain how to use categorizations discussed in Silver, Strong, and Perini (2007): Mastery, understanding, self-expression, interpersonal, and four-style. I have adapted (including using alternative names for some similar concepts) their descriptions of these best practices, and I have focused on their usefulness as math and science assessment strategies for average students.

Mastery-Based Assessment

Teams-Games-Tournaments Example

Here is a math example of this popular strategy that should work well with average students (Figure 4.5). (DeVries, Edwards, & Slavin, 1978; Silver, Strong, & Perini, 2007)

Figure 4.5.

Curriculum				
SCOS	**EQ**: What are important facts to remember for science or math?	**Know**—vocabulary terms for a specific math or science topic	**Understand** that practice and teamwork help us better remember important facts for science and math	**Do**—participate in a tournament to learn facts about a math or science topic *(See MO below)*

Measurable Objective				
Introduction	**Thinking Verbs**	**Product**	**Response Criterion**	**Content**
Students will...	recall	short answers	that are correct about	important science or math facts.

Differentiation		
Readiness—teacher-guided process	**Interests**—can allow students to choose the terms for review to increase interest in content. Earning points for a team also increases interest in achieving.	**Style**—interpersonal, mastery, visual, kinesthetic (pulling cards)

Procedures

Take these steps to set it up:

Step 1: Divide the class into groups as follows: Each group should have one relatively high functioning student, who is labeled "advanced," two or more middle functioning students who are labeled "average," and one low functioning student who is labeled "novice" or other innocuous designation. The teacher should limit the teams to four to make the competition flow more easily.

Step 2: Make a set of review cards for each table. An adaptation could be asking students to make the questions with the following directions: For math the questions should center on math vocabulary or problems that students can answer by doing the math in their heads. Make sure questions require one right answer and that they are numbered to correspond with the answer key that each table should also have.

Step 3: Appoint a group leader (the highest functioning student), who will help the students take turns and will check answers. Students practice answering the questions on the cards to prepare for the tournament.

Step 4: The tournament can be the same day as the practice or the next day depending on the amount of class time available. Make sure each table has a set of cards and a key. All questions and keys should be the same; however, the cards can be color coded to designate teams. The teams could choose their color in advance. They could also have a team name, and so on.

Step 5. When it is time for the tournament to begin, give the signal to the students designated "advanced" to go to the "advanced" table. Students designated "average" can go to one or more "average tables." The students designated "novice" go to the "novice table."

Step 6: Students proceed with the game as follows: Students take turns pulling a card from the stack of cards. The appointed or elected leader of the group checks to see that the student has answered the question correctly. This leadership role might rotate depending how often students play the game. Students earn points for their home group.

Step 7: After each table has gone through all the cards or if time has run out, players return to their home teams to tally and record their total points. The winning team is awarded an A; the second place team takes a B; and the other teams are awarded C. No one fails. The teacher can take a running total of team points to conduct a celebration at the end of the year and a special acknowledgement for winning teams.

Students enjoy this process, and the teacher gets a good idea of how much students are learning.

Understanding-Based Formative (or Summative) Assessment

Real-World Problem Solving Example

This strategy is an excellent way to formatively assess average students' learning because it shows how an academic topic applies to the real world. Figure 4.6 is a science example of this strategy.

Figure 4.6. Real-World Problem Solving—Science

Curriculum				
SCOS	**EQ**: What is the best process for solving a real-world problem?	**K**now—how to research a science topic to solve a real problem, how to construct a product (such as brochure, PowerPoint presentation, or booklet) to show how to solve the problem, more information about the topic related to the problem	**U**nderstand that research can help us find information to help solve important problems caused by chemical reactions in the real world	**D**o— *(See MO below)*

Measurable Objective				
Introduction	**Thinking Verbs**	**Product**	**Response Criterion**	**Content**
Students will…	generate, plan, produce, create, implement, organize, and evaluate	a solution to a real-world problem	that is an efficient, effective, creative, and reasonable	solution to real-world problems generated by chemical reactions.

Differentiation		
Readiness—check-points to assure students are proceeding as they should	**Interests**—students choose from a list of projects	**Style**—understanding, creative, investigative

Procedures

Average students would enjoy a chance to participate in a real-world problem-solving assessment process, but teachers must not make it too open-ended. Therefore, they could offer problem choices and give students specific guidelines for solving it. Figure 4.7 is an example of a syllabus teachers might use to solve a real-world science problem.

Figure 4.7. Science Example of a Real-World Problem

**Syllabus for Solving a Real-World Science Problem—
Chemical Reactions**

Step 1: Choose a problem from the ones listed below related to the unit on Chemical Reactions.

Problem 1: The elderly, children, and some sensitive adults are susceptible to the chemicals found in our buildings, in the atmosphere, and in our water supply. Find out which chemicals are most dangerous to these people and make a brochure, PowerPoint presentation, or booklet that might help them.

Problem 2: Every year fire destroys homes and kills people. Students learn fire safety as soon as they get to school, but we continue to have loss of property and loss of lives because people do not understand fire. Make a brochure, PowerPoint presentation, or booklet that you might show to a group of elementary students and their parents about fire and fire safety.

Problem 3: American teenagers are hooked on fast foods, but although these foods taste good, they contain unhealthy substances. Find out how the chemicals in fast foods affect those who eat them and design a brochure, PowerPoint presentation, or booklet to explain how dangerous they can be to the health of those who eat them.

Step 2: Find at least three sources of information to inform your work. Make sure to cite these sources in MLA form.

Step 3: What follows are the dates that parts of the project are due:

Date due: _____   Your decision about the problem you will address and where you plan to find information

Date due: _____   Notes you have taken on the topic

Date due: _____   Plan for the product

Date due: _____   Product

Use the attached rubric to make sure you are on the right track

---

Rubric for Real-World Science Problem: Chemical Reactions				
Criteria	Level 1	Level 2	Level 3	Level 4
Content	The amount of information included in the product does not sufficiently cover the topic and/or many of the facts are inaccurate.	The amount of information included in the product leaves out many important ideas and/or includes some ideas that are inaccurate.	The product includes enough ideas to adequately cover the topic, and all ideas are accurate.	The product includes in- depth and accurate information that exceeds the expectations for the product.
Organization	The information in the product appears to be arranged in a random manner.	The information in the product is arranged so that it is hard to follow and confusing.	The information in the product is well-organized and easy to follow.	The organization of the product matches exceptionally well with the information.
Style	The writing style is simple, has many grammati-cal errors, and is sloppy.	The writing style is uninteresting and often distracts from the ideas generated as the solution.	The writing style is adequate and expresses the ideas generated as the solution in a clear and concise manner.	The writing style creates interest and enthusiasm for the solution. The writing includes excellent uses of literary devices.
Originality	The information is taken directly from a source with no attempt to synthesize it.	The information is not presented in a way that differs much from the sources from which it was taken.	The product is creative and interesting and shows a synthesis of the information.	The product is very interesting and shows an exceptionally creative solution to the problem.

Note that for average students, the problem assessment should not be too open-ended, the teacher should require checkpoints to make sure students are proceeding as they should, and the rubric is written in terms that students should be able to understand (the teacher should make sure they do understand it by asking them to paraphrase it either orally or in writing.)

Self-Expression–Based Formative Assessment

Visualizing Example

This strategy can assess students' abilities to translate written or spoken words into pictures. Average students should already have some experience with this process but may need some encouragement and review to put visualization into practice. Visualizing facilitates two ways to think about a piece of information. It should help average students better visualize, remember, and understand important concepts and skills.

Figure 4.8 is a math lesson that assesses students' ability to visualize, remember, and understand "indirect measurement."

Figure 4.8. Math Example of Visualization—Indirect Measurement

Curriculum				
SCOS	**EQ**: How can we use ratio and proportion to estimate height?	**K**now—how to use visualizing, drawing, indirect measurement to determine the height of very tall objects	**U**nderstand that using visualization and ratios and proportions can help us determine the height of very tall things	**D**o—visualize, draw, and set up a ratio and proportion to determine the height of very tall objects *(See MO below)*

Measurable Objective				
Introduction	*Thinking Verbs*	*Product*	*Response Criterion*	*Content*
Students will…	exemplify and create	pictures and numbers	accurately depicting	the process of using indirect measurement.

Differentiation		
Readiness—teacher-guided process, teacher checks constantly for understanding while circulating around the room	**Interests**—students allowed to use creativity in their drawings	**Style**—self-expression, visual, creative, mathematical/logical

Procedures

Step 1: Explain to students that their ability to visualize and record that visualization on a piece of paper will be assessed. Hand each student an 8 × 10 inch piece of white paper, and make sure all students have pencils and possibly some means of coloring what they draw.

Step 2: Tell students that you will use a visualizing method to help them learn how to use proportions to find the dimensions of objects that are difficult to measure directly, and tell them that as you read, you want them to draw what they hear. Next tell them that they must first prepare the space for their drawing. Tell them to divide the paper into four boxes like Figure 4.9.

Figure 4.9. Indirect Measurement by—(student's name)

Problem 1	Problem 2
Problem 3	Problem 4

Model each of these steps and show students what the paper should look like. Next, ask them to title the picture "Indirect Measurement" and ask them to put their name beside the title. Tell them they are going to practice the process of visualizing and then drawing.

Step 5: Tell students you are going to read them a word problem and that they will learn to use indirect measurement.

Step 6: Read the following problem and ask students to draw what they hear.

A boy is looking up at a tall tree. He measures the shadow of the tree, which is about 6 feet long. The boy measures his own shadow, and it is about 2 feet long. The boy is 5 feet tall. How tall is the tree?

Step 7: Make sure the students are drawing the pictures. Prompt the students to make two triangles, one with the boy and his shadow and the other with the tree and its shadow. Make sure students are doing this correctly as in Figure 4.10.

Figure 4.10. The Boy and His Shadow

Tell students to label the sides of the triangles appropriately and then to set up a ratio as follows:

The person's shadow is 2 feet and goes over the tree's shadow, which is 6 feet. The person's height is 5 feet, and the tree's height is unknown, x, which is $2/6 = 5/x$. Solve for x, and $2x = 6 \times 5$, $2x = 30$, $x = 15$. Tell the students to note that the tree is approximately 15 feet tall.

Step 8: Give the students more word problems to draw and solve. Students should label the first picture "1," and label the next box, "2." They should get ready to draw the next problem.

Step 9: Students listen to each of the following word problems and follow the same process as the first problem:

Problem 2: A fire hydrant sits a few feet from an office building. The fire hydrant is about 2 feet tall, and its shadow is 1 foot long. The building's shadow is 10 feet. How tall is the building?

Problem 3: A father built an 8-foot-tall dollhouse for his children. The dollhouse shadow is 3 feet long, and the house has a 7-foot-long shadow. How tall is the house?

Problem 4: A cat sits next to a large flowering bush. The cat is 10 inches tall, and its shadow is 4 inches long. The flowering bush's shadow is 15 inches long. How tall is the flowering bush?

Step 10: After students have completed the drawings and solved them, the teacher should collect and evaluate the work. He or she may choose to give students a summative assessment to determine if students can use this process on their own to solve an indirect measurement problem.

Interpersonal-Based Assessment

Interpersonal-based assessments use students' natural inclination to help each other and work together. These kinds of assessments, if handled with some teacher guidance and prompting, should motivate average students.

Jigsaw Example

This cooperative learning assessment works well with average students. Here is an example of using jigsaw (Figure 4.11) as a way to assess students' learning a science topic (Aronson, et al., 1978).

Teachers should use this activity as they explore "materials" such as the following: polymers and composites, metals and alloys, ceramics and glass, and radioactive elements.

Figure 4.11. Jigsaw—Exploring Materials

Curriculum				
SCOS	**EQ**: How are they formed and how do we use various materials like polymers, metals, ceramics, glass, and radioactive elements in our lives?	**K**now—how various materials (e.g., polymers, metals, ceramics, glass, and radioactive elements) are formed, how they might be used in our lives, and what makes them useful.	**U**nderstand that…Various materials like polymers, metals, ceramic, glass, and radioactive elements have varying properties and important uses in our lives.	**D**o—read about and determine how materials are formed and how they might be useful. Plan how to teach the information to peers, teach the information, and assess the learning. (See MO below)

Measurable Objective				
Introduction	*Thinking Verbs*	*Product*	*Response Criterion*	*Content*
Students will…	summarize, compare, explain, organize, differentiate, plan, and produce	teaching materials	that adequately and accurately	explore how materials are formed and how they might be useful in our lives.

Differentiation		
Readiness—teacher-guided process	**Interests**—working in a group to learn together, choosing how to teach a topic	**Style**—interpersonal, investigative, visual, and auditory

Procedures

Step 1: Put each student in a home group and ask them to number off 1 through 4. If there are an uneven number of students, make a group of five. There may be several groups of four or five.

Step 2: Assign students who are number 4 (and 5) to read a selection about polymers and composites, assign students who are number 3 to read about metals and alloys, assign students who are number 2 to read about ceramics and glass, and assign students who are number 1 to read about radioactive elements.

Step 3: Instruct students to move to a 1 table, a 2 table, a 3 table and a 4 table. Tell students at each table that they should read their assignment and complete some products with which to teach their home group about their topic. Structure this activity by giving students blank white paper or poster paper, cards and markers so that they might construct some flashcards or posters that teach about their topic. Ask them to make a five-problem quiz to test their home group members' knowledge of their topic. Students should make a quiz for each member of their home group. The groups should have four or five members.

Step 4: When students return to their home groups, they should take turns teaching and assessing that group about their topic. They should give home group members the quiz they designed and submit grades to the teacher.

Four-Style Assessment

Window Notes Example

This is a way of assessing several aspects of what students are gaining from a lesson (Silver, Strong, Perini, & Tuculescu, 2003; Silver, Strong, & Perini, 2007). For window notes the teacher might assess the following: the facts students are recording, how they feel about that information, what questions they have about it, and what ideas they have about how they might use that topic.

Figure 4.12. Window Notes

Curriculum				
SCOS	**EQ**: Why is digestion important to good health?	**K**now—how to make notes in four ways on the subject of digestion	**U**nderstand that digestion is a complicated process that is essential for good health	**D**o—make notes based on facts, feelings, questions, and ideas *(See MO below)*

Measurable Objective				
Introduction	*Thinking Verbs*	*Product*	*Response Criterion*	*Content*
Students will…	summarize, produce, exemplify, attribute, generate, and implement	window notes	that accurately and thoroughly note facts, feelings, questions, and ideas	about digestion and pH.

Differentiation		
Readiness—teacher-guided process and graphic organizer	**Interests**—students choose the four aspects of the notes to take	**Style**—interpersonal, understanding, mastery, and self-expression

Procedures

Step 1: Announce that students will be taking notes about the lesson in a new way.

Step 2: Next hand out an 8 × 10 inch sheet of white paper that shows how to divide a sheet into four equal boxes.

Step 3: Ask students to label each of the boxes as follows:

- Facts
- Feelings
- Questions
- Ideas

Step 4: Ask students to write in the boxes they have created, as you talk about the topic.

The following is a science example on digestion and pH. It begins at Step 5 of the previously explained procedures for this assessment.

Window Notes on Digestion and pH

Step 5: Assuming Steps 1 through 4 are completed, now explain that the class will be learning about digestion. For average students, the exercise could be for students to eat something to notice how it tastes and then to answer the question, "What is digestion?"

Step 6: Instruct the students to read about digestion in their textbook or another text. Instruct students to collect facts, feelings, questions, and ideas in the correct boxes as they come to them.

For this Window Note, students should find at least seven facts, seven feelings, seven questions, and seven ideas. Allow students to share one at a time from each of the four boxes. Collect the work for evaluation but return it to students so that they may keep it in a notebook for studying purposes.

With all of these assessments, it is important to rotate them so that students have an opportunity to experience each type of assessment.

Summative Assessments for Average Students

Most textbooks provide summative assessments for teachers to use, and these assessments should be fair for average students; however, the teacher may want to evaluate any summative assessment based on the criteria in Chapter 2.

Constructing Summative Assessments for Average Students

Teachers may use textbook-generated true/false, short answer, matching, and multiple choice tests because the textbook levels them for average students. However, teachers should evaluate these textbook resources based on the criteria listed in Chapter 2 and keep in mind that these tests may not always fit the needs of the class; therefore, they may need to construct their own tests. Keeping in mind that these types of tests, especially multiple choice, align with high-stakes testing, makes familiarizing students with their "grammar" important. Until, or if, the present culture of accountability through multiple choice, norm-based, standardized testing, ceases to be, students should have practice throughout the year showing what they know though multiple choice assessments. Teachers need to make sure their multiple choice classroom assessments align with the high stakes tests.

Extended-Writing Response

To make these kinds of assessments fair for average students, teachers should make sure they can check off the criteria found in Chapter 2. What follows are some writing prompts for math and science. Notice that the prompts are somewhat longer for average students than for at-risk students.

Procedures

The following are math essay prompts for average students.

1. The educational leaders who oversee the curriculum for elementary through high school require that all students study mathematics. Explain why you think these decision makers made that decision and how their decision affects you.

2. We have just recently finished learning how to solve equations, and you have seen several real-world applications related to sports, recreational activities, the weather, and others. Of all the applications you have seen, which one is most important to you and why?

3. Scientists and mathematicians find many uses for tables and graphs. Think of a real-world use for tables and graphs and explain the advantages or disadvantages of using them to solve this problem.

4. The study of mathematics (geometry, algebra) includes many rules and laws that make solving problems easier. Choose one of the rules or laws and explain how that rule or law makes solving a real-world problem much easier than without that rule or law.

The following are science essay prompts for average students.

1. Scientists have important roles in advancing medical care. Think of an important scientific discovery that has made a remarkable difference in medical care and explain in detail how that discovery has affected the lives of people around the world.

2. Math and science share many of the same tools, such as graphs and charts. Think of a specific tool and explain how you might use one of them to examine the ocean. Make sure to give specific examples of how you would use this tool for a specific reason.

3. Explain in a detailed essay how plant and animal cells are different and alike. Make sure to compare and contrast them with regard to their structure, functions, and processes.

4. Write an informational essay explaining the history of _____ (a specific area of science) and include how that history is important to present discoveries or advances.

For average students, it is important that students plan their work using a graphic organizer. Teachers may actually look at the plan first to determine if students are on the right track before they take time writing an essay. See Chapter 3 for a generic graphic organizer for expository (nonfiction) writing and including persuasion.

Projects and Performances

Average students enjoy doing projects; however, they need to show the teacher that they are completing their work in a timely manner. The teacher should plan checkpoints along the way.

One of the best projects to assign average students is an inquiry-based self-selected project based on a topic within a unit of study. The project can be assigned as homework to supplement the work the students are doing in class to learn about the topic, or students can do it as an in-class experiential assessment process. Because it is inquiry-based, the teacher must make sure students understand how to cite sources and how to avoid plagiarism. Figure 4.13 shows a generic inquiry-based project syllabus.

Figure 4.13. Generic Inquiry-Based Project Syllabus

You may complete this project individually, with a partner, or with a small group (no more than five to a group).

1. Choose a topic within our unit of study that you would like to explore in more depth. Due date: _____.

2. Find a minimum of _____ *(teacher decides the number based on time limits and level of students)* sources. Sources might include primary sources, such as interviews and primary documents or secondary sources, such as accounts in encyclopedias and books written about the topic. Due date: _____

3. Take notes from your sources and think about how you might best show your knowledge of the topic. Go over the Project Rubric to make sure you understand how your work will be evaluated. Due date: _____

4. Choose a product from this list or propose your own:
   - ♦ An informational paper
   - ♦ A children's book
   - ♦ A creative story based on the information about the topic.
   - ♦ A pictorial explanation of the topic (drawings or photos), including written information about each picture.
   - ♦ A movement or dance based on the information you gather about the topic. (Requires a commentary explaining the movements.)
   - ♦ A live or filmed documentary or skit (with people or puppets) based on the topic.
   - ♦ A taped or live radio play or talk show based on the topic.
   - ♦ A PowerPoint presentation about the topic.
   - ♦ A three-dimensional display about the topic, including written commentary.

5. Organize your information based on the project you choose and make a "Works Cited" page to show the sources you used to inform your project. Due date: _____

6. Explain your plan on the "Project Proposal" form. (See below) Due date: _____

7. Meet with the teacher to go over your plan. Due date: _____

8. Work on your project.

9. Sign up to present it and present it. Due date:_____

10. Accept feedback and evaluation from peers and from the teacher.

    Note that there are check points that are due along the way and that the syllabus includes several suggested products.

Figure 4.14. Project Proposal

Name(s): _____

Name of project: _____

Type of project (For example: film, PowerPoint presentation): _____

List sources of information:

  1.

  2.

  3.

_____ Check here if your "Works Cited" page is complete.

Learning objectives your project will address:

  1.

  2.

Time you need to present project: _____

Supplies and equipment you need for your project (For example, projector, poster paper):

Other comments:

When teachers meet with students, they should go over the Project Proposal form (Figure 4.14) with them to make sure they are on the right track. They should also make sure students have completed their "Works Cited" page correctly and that they understand the rubric (Figure 4.15).

Figure 4.15. Project Holistic Rubric

Level 1: Project information lacks depth and/or accuracy and does not show evidence of sufficient learning about the topic. It is poorly organized and lacks evidence of preparation. There is weak evidence of researched information supporting the project, and much of it is well-known and/or copied from sources. The project lacks creativity, originality, and completeness. There is little to no audience awareness.

Level 2: Project information is superficial and at times inaccurate. There is some evidence of learning, but it is not extensive. The organization of the project does not add to its overall effect. There is little evidence of time spent to prepare it. Research is evident; however, it is superficial and overly dependent on prior knowledge and ideas that are elementary. The project shows some evidence of creativity, but that creativity is not well-aligned with the information or the learning objectives. Although there is some audience awareness, it is superficial.

Level 3: Project information is sufficient and accurate. The project clearly addresses the learning objectives and provides new ideas that go beyond students' prior knowledge and superficial information. Organization supports the overall effect of the project. Creativity is organic to the information the project presents. The project demonstrates a sense of audience awareness.

Level 4: Project information is extensive and accurate. The project supplies new ideas that go well-beyond students' prior knowledge and superficial information. The project shows evidence of a great deal of preparation and in-depth research. Organization enhances the delivery of the information. Creativity and originality are obvious and well-integrated with facts. The project shows a complex synthesis of the intended learning objectives. The project is highly successful in its connection with the audience.

Summary

Average students are the easiest to assess because most of them read at grade level and should respond to grade-level texts and activities. They should also have social skills that allow them to work in groups so that they might enjoy the learning process.

5

Math and Science Enrichment Assessments

Academically gifted or advanced students have special assessment needs for which teachers should plan if they want to appropriately challenge them. As teachers begin to think about how to plan assessments for gifted or highly advanced students, they need to have a clear understanding of how these students think and behave.

This chapter shows teachers specific examples of differentiated assessment strategies that are leveled for students who are gifted or highly advanced. After providing an overview of these students' special needs, the chapter includes examples of preassessments, formative assessments, and summative assessments. For the formative assessments, there is information about the Differentiating Assessment: Six-Part Template. What follows is a thorough explanation of Part 1 of the Differentiating Assessment: Six-Part Template for students who may need enrichment assessments.

Students Needs: Who Are These Students Who Need Enrichment Assessments?

To design effective assessments for gifted or highly advanced students, teachers need to keep in mind some of their strengths that might cause problems for teachers as they plan assessments for them. Figure 5.1 is a chart that shows how the social, emotional, and academic strengths of gifted students can cause problems for them and their teachers.

Figure 5.1. Social, Emotional, and Academic Strengths of Gifted Students

Strengths	Possible Resulting Assessment Issues
They learn information much more quickly than others and may in some cases actually be able to learn faster than all or some of their teachers.	They may become impatient with their peers or their teachers. They may get bored with the pace of the assessments if teachers base it on the needs of average students or their own learning pace.
They constantly ask questions and look for significance.	They may ask what appear to be inappropriate questions and may want to explore an issue in more depth than the rest of the class.
They are intrinsically motivated to learn.	They may resist teachers' form of assessment, especially if they rely too much on extrinsic rewards.
They prefer assessments that allow them to show how they can solve problems, think abstractly, and synthesize information.	They are not as responsive to assessments that are standardized or that do not allow them to show their abilities.
They are highly concerned with fairness.	Assessments based on humanitarian concerns motivate them. They may challenge the teacher's fairness in some assessments.
They like to organize things and people.	They can seem bossy and critical of others when they are participating in a group assessment process.
They have vocabularies that outstrip the average person's.	They may use those words to manipulate or to challenge, which makes it more difficult for them to participate in assessments with average or at-risk students.
They have extremely high expectations of themselves.	They are often disappointed in themselves and others when they are not perfect. They may be obsessed with making the highest grades and scores on assessments. These expectations can interfere with their ability to participate in group assessments. Teachers may have to deal with their depression and sullenness if they do not achieve at highest levels.

They are creative and like to do things in different ways.	They may not respond well to unimaginative assessments and may seem out of step with others.
They can concentrate intensely for long periods.	They may choose assessment projects that cause them to neglect everything but that assessment.
They are more sensitive to criticism than others are.	They may not respond well to any negative teacher or peer feedback they might get for an assessment.
They are highly energetic and eager to use their minds.	They may appear hyperactive if teachers require them to endure assessments that bore them.
They are independent nonconformists.	They may prefer individualized assessments and may not prefer group assessments.
Their interests are varied, and they tend to use divergent thinking.	They may need teacher direction to stay focused on the goals of an assessment.

Adapted from http://www.kidsource.com/kidsource/content2/social_development_gifted.html,

Knowing these things about gifted and highly advanced students, teachers must maintain sensitivity toward them if they want to give them the best chance of showing what they know.

How Learner Outcomes for Gifted and Highly Advanced Students Differ from Generic Outcomes

To make it clear that assessing gifted and highly advanced students differs quite a bit from assessing at-risk or average students, the following chart (Figure 5.2) provides an excellent overview of science learning goals for average students and those set for gifted or highly advanced students.

Figure 5.2. Science Learning Goals

Average Students	*Gifted Students*
Comprehend the major concepts included in the unit.	Evaluate diverse materials according to a set of criteria.
Are familiar with the structural elements of the cell.	Create a self-selected product related to the important structural elements of the cell.
Develop an understanding of the parts of the plant and animal cell.	Analyze and interpret the functions of plant cells and animal cells in medical research.

These ideas were adapted from http://www.kidsourse.come/kidsource/content/learner_outcomes.html

From this comparison it is obvious that assessments for gifted or highly advanced students are much more challenging, broader, and focused on higher-level thinking skills. Those who assess gifted and highly advanced students assume that these students can read and comprehend information above their grade level and that differentiating assessment is critical if teachers want to address their assessment needs.

Math and Science Examples of Preassessments: Content

Anticipation Guide

What follows is a science example of an Anticipation Guide for gifted or highly advanced students. Note how the guide includes high level science vocabulary and requires students to infer.

Procedures

Step 1: Hand out the Anticipation Guide and then ask students to find the answers in a text.

Step 2: Students may complete the process individually, with a partner, or in a small group.

Step 3: After the students have responded to the guide, make a list with the whole class showing how many students agreed or disagreed with the statement.

Step 4: Students read the text to correct their answers.

Step 5: Conduct another whole-class discussion about the correct answers.

Note: The following Anticipation Guide 3 (Figure 5.3)provides an example of how teachers might take the same process (anticipation guide) and level it for three readiness levels.

Figure 5.3. Matter: Anticipation Guide 3

Read the statements below and decide if you agree (A) or disagree (D) with each statement. Write your answers in the left column under "Anticipation." After you have learned about the topic, complete the right column under "Reaction." Notice what you have learned.

Anticipation	Statement	Reaction
	1. At room temperature, propane is a liquid.	
	2. To observe the chemical properties of a substance, you must try to change it in some way.	
	3. Chemical formulas show the ratio of one element to another.	
	4. A homogeneous mixture is made of many different parts.	
	5. There are only four ways to separate the components of a mixture: magnetic attraction, filtration, distillation, and evaporation.	
	6. Seawater is a mixture.	
	7. Helium has no chemical properties.	
	8. Melting point is a chemical property.	
	9. The holes in bread come from air pockets.	
	10. Everything is matter.	

Key: 1. D; 2. A; 3. A; 4. D; 5. D; 6. A; 7. D; 8. A; 9. D; 10. A.

Interview

Gifted or highly advanced students may enjoy this strategy. They have the social skills to stay focused on the topic and to take it seriously. Teachers might give students an interview template or ask them to make their own interview format. Teachers should then ask them to move around the room (the teacher could specify a certain amount of steps they should take to connect with their first interviewee) to find out what at least three students in the class already know about the topic. Students should report and then turn in their findings so that the teacher can get a better idea about what they already know. The teacher may teach these students to use Accountable Talk. See Chapter 3 for an explanation.

Informal Assessments

Math and Science Examples of Informal Assessments

Teachers can informally assess gifted and highly advanced students by using the methods described in Chapter 2. Teachers might also use impromptu "multiple intelligences assessments" to determine if these students understand math concepts.

Procedures

Have a box of costumes, balls of string, hats, props, white paper, markers, glue stick, a CD or tape player, and a keyboard or other instrument available for these assessments. When a new math or science concept is introduced, ask individuals, student partners, or small groups (no more than three to a group) to interpret these concepts for the class.

- ◆ Math example: Introduce the concept, "central tendency" and give students a short period of time (10–15 minutes) to use one of these intelligences: kinesthetic (dance, skit, commercial, puppet show), visual art (drawing, painting), or musical (song or rap) to show their understanding of "central tendency."

- ◆ Science example: Use the same process with the concept, "topographic maps."

Formative Assessments

Formative assessments allow teachers to determine if their students are learning what the teacher is teaching them. What follows are several examples of differentiated formative assessment strategies that will help the teacher enrich assessment for gifted or highly advanced students.

Differentiating Assessment: Six-Part Template—Parts 2 through 5

For each assessment example, teachers will see examples of how to address Parts 2 through 5 of Differentiating Assessment: Six-Part Template. The first part of this chapter covered Part 1 for all examples, and teachers can only complete Part 6 after they have implemented the assessment. Figure 5.4 is a review of the template for this process.

Figure 5.4. Differentiating Assessment: Six-Part Template

1. Students' Needs–described in detail				
2. Curriculum				
Standard course of study (**SCOS**)	Essential Question (**EQ**)	**K**now	**U**nderstand	**D**o *(See MO below)*
3. Measurable Objective				
Introduction	Thinking Verbs	Product	Response Criterion	Content
4. Differentiation				
Readiness		Interests		Learning Styles
5. Assessment Procedures (listed by steps)				
6. Assessment Audit				

Differentiated Formative Assessments by Learning Styles

For the assessment strategies that follow, I use the differentiated and strategic categorizations discussed in Silver, Strong, and Perini (2007): mastery, understanding, self-expression, interpersonal, and four-style. I have adapted (including using alternative names for some similar concepts) their descriptions of these best practices, and I have focused on enriching the aspect of their usefulness as math and science assessment strategies for gifted and highly advanced students.

Mastery-Based Formative Assessments

Direct Instruction Example

This strategy, which is updated Madeline Hunter by Robin Hunter (2004) allows for constant formative assessment during guided practice and independent practice (Figure 5.5). When using this type of assessment with gifted or highly advanced students, the teacher must keep in mind that these students absorb information much more quickly and need less guided practice than at-risk or average students; therefore, the teacher might replace guided practice with "facilitated" practice and troubleshooting.

**Figure 5.5. Math or Science Integrated Example
of Direct Instruction Assessment**

Curriculum				
SCOS	**EQ:** How can we use a rate of change formula to organize important data into a useful graph?	**K**now—how to solve a science or math problem by collecting data over time to use a rate of change formula that creates a graph. How to draw conclusions about collected data.	**U**nderstand that a rate of change formula can help organize important data into a useful graph	**D**o— solve a math or science problem by collecting data to use in a rate of change formula that is shown on a graph. Draw conclusions about collected data. *(See MO below)*

Measurable Objective				
Introduction	**Thinking Verbs**	**Product**	**Response Criterion**	**Content**
Students will...	interpret, apply, create, and produce	their choice of a problem	that demonstrates a thorough and accurate	solution using application of the rate of change formula.

Differentiation		
Readiness—syllabus	**Interests**—choice of topic and style	**Style**—various styles from which students may choose, mastery

Procedures

Because this is an integrated assessment, the math and science teachers can provide the optimal learning experience if they plan the assessment together.

Modeling: Either the math or the science teacher models a lesson, showing how collecting data on a science topic and using a "rate of change formula" allows them to make informative visual representations, such as line graphs, to better show their data. As a direct instruction assessment process, the teacher might use the following modeling strategies to present the problem:

- *Visual:* Using an example of a scientist gathering data about plant growth using a change formula to plot the growth of hybrid plants he or she is testing as possible sources of fuel. This presentation could be a PowerPoint presentation or posters and handouts.

- *Oral:* Explain how to set up the comparison data, plug it into the formula, and then plot the information on a graph.

- *Kinesthetic:* Ask students to take notes or act out the example above so that they might use their notes to solve or create a similar problem on their own. (By having students take notes and assessing those notes, the teacher can tell if students comprehend the process so that they might use it for their own problem.)

Assessment: Guided practice—Give students a choice among several science problems to which they might apply the rate of change formula and plot the information on a graph. Act as a coach to help students solve the problems. Students present their findings to the class, which increases learning opportunities. Figure 5.6 shows some suggested problem choices.

Figure 5.6. Problem Choices

1. If a bacterium undergoes reproduction by binary fission every 20 minutes, and the new cells survive to reproduce at the same rate, draw a graph that represents the number of bacterial cells that would grow from a single bacterium within 3 hours. Also write an explanation of binary fission. *(Logical/mathematical)*

2. Explore the process of evaporation by doing an experiment in which you determine the rate at which a beaker of water might empty when you boil it. Start your time when the water begins boiling. Write an explanation of the process of evaporation and boiling point. *(Kinesthetic)*

3. Show the rate of change in the number of people affected by a major health issue (such as AIDS or sexually transmitted diseases [STDs]) using labeled artistic representations (pictures) rather than a line graph. Write an explanation of your pictures and numbers. *(Artistic)*

4. Work with a group to construct a human line graph showing the rate of change in the carbon emissions generated from a television over 8 hours of use. *(Interpersonal and kinesthetic)*

5. Write your analysis of four science-based graphs supplied by the teacher that show the rate of change. *(Analytical/rational)*

Independent practice: Give gifted or highly advanced students a homework assignment that deepens their knowledge of "rate of change." The students may do the work on their own, with a partner, or with a small group (Figure 5.7). Note that gifted and highly advanced students seem to have fewer problems getting together with others outside of class and giving them projects with which they might work with others can become an excellent socialization opportunity for students who have issues with making friends.

Figure 5.7. Independent Practice Problem

Find a problem in science that requires the following:

Collection of data over time

Use of the rate of change formula and graphing.

Requirements:

Collect data from your problem/experiment.

Create a rate of change graph on a poster or in a PowerPoint presentation.

Explain your findings in writing and orally in a presentation.

Holistic project standards:

Level 1—D	Level 2—C	Level 3—B	Level 4—A
Data is inaccurate in places. Science topic is elementary and mostly common knowledge. Visuals are sloppy, disorganized, and insufficient.	Data is mostly accurate with some inaccuracies. Science topic is on grade level, but coverage is minimal. Visuals are organized and neat but do not have a sense of originality.	Data is accurate. Science topic is on grade level and includes sufficient details. Visuals are organized and neat. The project is original and creative.	Data is accurate and extensive. Science topic is above grade level. It is highly complex and detailed. The project is organized neat, highly original, and creative. It has an over all effect of "Wow!"

Understanding-Based Formative Assessment

Concept Attainment Example

This strategy includes assessing students' abilities to explore in depth what complex words might mean (Bruner, 1973) (Figure 5.8). Gifted or highly advanced students might learn a great deal about complex concepts using Jerome Bruner's process of "concept attainment."

Figure 5.8.

Curriculum				
SCOS	**EQ:** How can understanding similarities and differences help us understand equations?	**K**now—how to use concept development to better understand the "equation"	**U**nderstand that an equation is a useful mathematical problem-solving tool that includes one or more variables	**D**o—categorize, identify similarities and differences, draw conclusions *(See MO below)*

Measurable Objective				
Introduction	**Thinking Verbs**	**Product**	**Response Criterion**	**Content**
Students will…	generate, classify, compare, organize	an organized list	that defines in detail	the concept, equation.

Differentiation		
Readiness—teacher modeling	**Interests**—students find their own examples	**Style**—understanding, mathematical/logical, analytical

Procedures

Figure 5.9 is an example of Jerome Bruner's "concept attainment" with a math example.

Figure 5.9. Bruner's Concept Attainment—Math Example

Step 1: Select a concept that is useful to both math and science learning, for example, help students explore the concept "equation." Next determine attributes that would fit under the "no" and the "yes" column. Make cards that are large enough for the student to see with one of the attributes listed on each card. Cards for this example would look like the following and have tape on the backs so that they can be attached to the chart.

Mathematical sentence that uses an equal sign: =

Positive examples are as follows: Includes one or more variables, $c = 12x$, useful in physics to predict how a ball will bounce, includes one or more inequalities, can be used to find the average annual precipitation.

Negative examples are as follows: $9 + x$, $x > y$, everyday language, a number line, $0.50 = 50\%$.

Step 2: Hand out the following worksheet so that students might record what is happening on the board.

Concept Attainment
Student Worksheet

Student's Name: _____

Yes	No

Step 3: Show the cards one at a time to the students. For the first card, "a mathematical sentence that uses an equal sign," say, "This card is a 'Yes.'" For the next card, which says, "9 + x," say "This card is a 'No.'" Repeat this process until there are three examples on the board.

Step 4: Ask students to look at the "Yes" column and ask what the cards have in common. Tell students not to say out loud what they notice.

Step 5: Hold up the next three cards and ask students to say in which column they should go. Some students will get it, and others may not. Ask students to offer more examples and prompt them to reveal the concept, which is "equations."

Step 6: Facilitate a discussion among students so that they might evaluate the process and talk about how they might apply it to future concept attainment activities.

Adapted from http://www.csus.edu/indiv/p/pfeiferj/EdTe226/concept%20attainment/ca_form.doc, accessed April 12, 2008.

Self-Expression–Based Formative Assessment

Metaphorical Expression or Synectics Example

Gifted or highly advanced students can make great use of this form of assessment, which evaluates their ability to make meaning through a creative process of comparison. Figure 5.10 is a math example showing how the teacher might assess gifted or highly advanced students using the synectics process (Gordon, 1961; Silver, Strong, & Perini, 2007).

Figure 5.10. Synectics—Parabola

Curriculum				
SCOS	**EQ:** How are emotions like parabolas? How are parabolas like emotions?	**K**now—how to brainstorm connections between two unlike things to note metaphorical connections, create products that connect two unlike concepts: concept of parabolas and feelings	**U**nderstand that we can compare two unlike concepts to help us deepen our understanding and knowledge of both of them	**D**o—Use the synectics process to deepen our understanding of two unlike concepts *(See MO below)*

Measurable Objective				
Introduction	**Thinking Verbs**	**Product**	**Response Criterion**	**Content**
Students will…	generate, compare, create, and critique	metaphorical statements and creative products	that expand and enhance	understanding of parabolas and emotions.

Differentiation		
Readiness—guiding through a process	**Interests**—students brainstorm and draw from their own experiences and interests	**Style**—self-expression, analytical, creative

Procedures

In each step, the teacher or designated student records the remarks of students as they brainstorm. The teacher makes it clear to students that no answer is silly or stupid and no one should criticize or make negative remarks about any remark.

Step 1: *Introduce the topic:* What is a parabola? Record all answers students might give about parabolas. Answers could be as follows: a curve, the graph of a quadratic function, has symmetry, has a vertex at its highest or lowest point, when the vertex is the minimum or lowest part of the parabola it opens upward, when the vertex is the maximum or highest point the parabola opens downward. Elicit deeper conceptualizations by asking questions, such as: When do we use parabolas? How do we graph them? Draw some lines on graph paper that are or are not parabolas to help students practice identifying them.

Step 2: *Create an analogy:* How is a parabola like emotions? Both have shape, both have cause and effect, both have direction, both can show upward movement (a smile) and downward movement (a frown), both have symmetry in terms of opposites, both can be pointed or flat, both have functions that shape them. Ask students to visualize and feel how a parabola might be like emotions. A sad parabola, a happy parabola, a parabola that shows pointed feelings, a parabola that shows blunted feelings, a parabola that shows opposite feeling, a quadratic function that creates a happy parabola, one that creates a pointed emotion, actions that like functions create emotion, such as an argument with a friend, which has many variables can create a downward emotional picture.

Step 3: Ask students to draw one of the analogies on a sheet of paper. For example a parabola that shows opposites of emotion, a parabola that shows heightened emotions, a parabola that shows dulled emotions. Ask students to also write the quadratic function that creates the parabola and use pictures to illustrate the variables that create the emotional picture.

Step 4: Students explore as a whole class discussion or with a partner how some of the words they have listed seem to be in conflict:

- "Pointed" and "flat" show conflicting emotions and conflicting quadratic functions.
- "Direction," "cause and effect," and "nonlinear" show how a parabola and an emotion can have direction and show cause and effect but can move in a nonlinear manner.

Step 5: *Create a new analogy.* Students propose new analogies and vote on one based on their drawings and performances. For example, students could decide that the best new analogy compares lines and emotions that do not move in a straight direction.

Step 6: Look for words or phrases that "redefine" parabola and that make learning about them a richer experience. For example, when we create parabolas from quadratic functions, we can see how they move in an upward or downward, pointed or flat direction, and we can associate that movement with our emotional lives. Also, when we think of our emotions we can think about how a quadratic function is like a series of events that create a parabola showing an upward or downward picture, just like our faces show upward or downward look on our faces. Finally, when we think of a graph as the context of our experiences, we can think of the parabola's location on that graph we might attach that location with an emotional state. Here are some suggestions for assessment products:

- Graph the parabolas for four quadratic equations. *(Supplied by the teacher or in the textbook.)* Write a short composition explaining how the parabolas are similar and different. Use "feeling" words to help you write your comparison paper.

- Create pictures of the variables for at least four quadratic functions and show the parabolas they will create.

- Write a report on how a quadratic function and its parabola might apply to a psychological or sociological issue.

- Create a graphic organizer that analyzes in detail how parabola and emotions are similar and different.

- Create a film about "The Parabola That Wouldn't Change."

Interpersonal-Based Assessment

Interpersonal-based assessments use students' natural inclination to help each other and work together; therefore, gifted or highly advanced students may enjoy these unless they are social isolates. In that case the teacher may need to use curriculum compacting or some other individualized contracting with them. See Northey (2005) for ideas on "curriculum compacting" and "individualizing instruction."

Jigsaw Example

This cooperative learning assessment works well with gifted or highly advanced students, who can use this activity with very little practice or teacher modeling. Figure 5.11 is an example of using jigsaw as a way to assess students' learning a math topic (Aronson, et al., 1978; Silver, Strong, & Perini, 2007).

Usually teachers use the jigsaw strategy to divide a long reading selection among a group of students. What follows is a way to use this strategy to review for a unit math test, for example, "solving and applying proportions."

Figure 5.11. Adapted Math Jigsaw

Curriculum				
SCOS	**EQ:** How might we use ratios and proportions to solve real-world situations?	**K**now—the process of using proportions to solve percent problems, how to find percent of change, how to find theoretical probability, how to find the probability of in-dependent events	**U**nderstand that students can use ratios and proportions to solve real-world situations	**D**o—solve and apply proportions, teach peers a specific math skill *(See MO below)*

Measurable Objective				
Introduction	**Thinking Verbs**	**Product**	**Response Criterion**	**Content**
Students will…	summarize, compare, explain, organize, differentiate, plan, and produce	teaching materials	that adequately and accurately	show how to use proportions to solve percent problems, how to find percent of change, how to find theoretical probability, and how to find the probability of independent events.

Differentiation		
Readiness—teacher facilitation	**Interests**—students choose interesting ways to teach	**Style**—logical and mathematical, creative, interpersonal

Procedures

Step 1: Put student's in a home group and ask them to number off 1 through 4. If there is an uneven number of students make a group of five students. There can be several groups of four or five.

Step 2: Use the "chapter review" problems in the textbook or make up your own. Each set of problems should represent a discreet portion of the unit, for example, assign students who are number 4 (and 5) the section of problems on "finding the probability of independent events." Assign students who are number 3 the section of problems on "using proportions when solving percent problems." Assign students who are number 2 the section of problems on "finding the percent of change." Assign students who are number 1 the section of problems on "finding the theoretical probability."

Step 3: Instruct students to move to a "1" table, a "2" table, a "3" table, or a "4" table. Tell students that they should work together to review and then solve at least five problems that exemplify their assigned section of the problems. These new groups should discuss how they might help the members of their "home group" review or relearn the skills they need to solve each type of problem within the unit. Provide blank white paper or poster paper, cards and markers so that students might construct some flashcards or posters that teach about their topic. Require each group to make a five-problem quiz to test their home group members' knowledge of their math skill. They should make a quiz for each member of their home group, which should have four or five members.

Step 4: When students return to their home groups they should take turns teaching their home group about their topic. Collect the student-made quizzes to determine if students have learned the material.

Four-Style Assessment

Circle of Knowledge Example

Circle of knowledge assessment is also known as seminar, Socratic seminar, or dialogic learning assessment (Silver, Strong, & Perini, 2007). This is a method of assessing students orally, and it works extremely well with gifted or highly advanced; it seems to be the kind of assessment "made" for gifted or advanced students. They thrive on it, and most of the time the teacher does not have to be concerned with assigning seats. If students talk to their neighbors too much, seats can be moved.

Unlike the community discussions described previously, this strategy allows the teacher to assess academic learning that is "tied to a text." What follows is an example of a seminar experience for gifted or highly advanced students, starting with a process useful to both math and science and finishing with a science example (Figure 5.12).

**Figure 5.12. Seminar Assessment—
General and Science Technology Example**

Curriculum				
SCOS	**EQ:** Can the Internet have harmful effects on our society?	**K**now—how to connect feelings and thoughts to high-level open-ended topics, how to express themselves orally	**U**nderstand the effects of the Internet on our society	**D**o—express feelings, thoughts, and values in a safe environment, connect personal feelings with a specific text, learn to support opinions with detailed information *(See MO below)*

Measurable Objective				
Introduction	**Thinking Verbs**	**Product**	**Response Criterion**	**Content**
Students will…	explain, summarize, produce, exemplify, attribute, and generate	oral responses	that are respectful, of others, thorough, accurate, and reference the text	about science technology.

Differentiation		
Readiness—teacher facilitation and practice	**Interests**—students connect with their own feelings and generate their own thoughts about this highly interesting and relevant topic	**Style**—open-ended, creative, interpersonal

Seminar Science Technology Example

Step 1: Ask students to read an essay called, "The Internet, Computer Games, and Morality" (Wu, 1999; Strong, et al., 1995) from "Ethics, Technology and Science," which is an award winning ThinkQuest. Note: Teachers can find a wealth of resources that are sure to interest gifted or highly advanced students on the ThinkQuest.org website. Their library of award-winning ThinkQuests is worth checking out at www.thinkquest.org/library.

Step 2: Explain to students how to write Level 2 and 3 questions. Here are some Level 2 examples for this essay:

- Do violent video games negatively affect children and teenagers?
- Why is the Internet anarchistic?
- How can the Internet be unethical?
- Which examples of Internet immorality are most dangerous?

Here are some Level 3 examples:

- What does the Internet teach us about responsible science?
- How could the Internet be useful to promote morality?
- Is morality always a choice?
- How might parents protect their children from Internet immorality?
- Which aspects of the Internet are most threatening to our society?

Follow the general rules and expectations for the remainder of this process.

Mini-Seminar:
An Adaptation of Whole Class Seminar

To offer a chance for even more intense conversation about a topic, teachers may want to divide the class in half, into medium-sized groups, or into groups of four or five. Note that teachers should only use this method after students have practiced the whole-class method of seminar discussion. To use this adapted version of seminar, teachers should take the following steps:

Step 1: Choose the content and a method of developing questions for seminar. Supply the questions or require students to generate them.

Step 2: Decide how to group the students. Here are some suggestions:

- Divide the class in half. Have one group of quiet and perhaps shy students and another group of more outgoing and verbal students.
- Divide the class into thirds based on learning styles.
- Form heterogeneous groups of four or five, making sure each group has a strong student leader and a good mix of abilities.

Step 3: Make sure each group has a leader and a recorder. Appoint these leaders or the students can elect them.

Step 4: Give these instructions:

1. The group leader will keep the discussion going. He or she will ask questions and allow others to ask them.

2. The recorder should record on a sheet of paper the names of each member of the group leaving three or four spaces between the names. The recorder's job is to put a slash mark (/) each time a student makes a comment. It is the recorder's responsibility to make sure all students get credit for contributing to the conversation.

3. I will grade you each on the number of comments you make that add to the conversation.

4. Are there any questions? You may begin.

Step 5: Constantly circulate to assure that the discussions are going smoothly. Encourage groups to give each student a chance to talk. Most gifted or highly advanced students take this process seriously and participate well. If a student does not take this seriously, remove him or her from the process and provide an alternative assignment.

Step 6: Evaluate this assessment by counting the number of comments each student makes in comparison with other members of the group. For example some groups have students who make detailed remarks; therefore, their recorder may have recorded fewer comments. Adjust the grading to match the style of the group.

With all of these assessments, it is important to rotate them so that students have an opportunity to experience each type of assessment.

Summative Assessments for Gifted or Highly Advanced Students

Most textbooks provide summative assessments for teachers to use with gifted or advanced students; however, they should find assessments for gifted or highly advanced students that challenge them beyond what average or at-risk students might be able to do. The critical issues for summative assessments for gifted or highly advanced students are as follows:

♦ They should not be required to do more questions than other students, but their questions might be more open-ended.

♦ Sometimes convergent test questions do not allow gifted or highly advanced student to do what they do so well, and that is divergent thinking. For example, some gifted and highly advanced student do poorly on "one-right-answer" tests because they overanalyze and see too many possibilities to settle on the one-right-answer the testmaker decided was correct.

Constructing Summative Assessments for Gifted or Highly Advanced Students

For gifted or highly advanced students, summative assessments for content should be more challenging, and the wording of the question stem should move as high up the thinking taxonomy as the question style will allow. Of the four listed here, multiple-choice questions might be the easiest to make higher level:

- ♦ True/false tests
- ♦ Short answer
- ♦ Multiple choice
- ♦ Matching
- ♦ Word puzzles: Allowing students to use a website to construct crossword or other word puzzles for each other can be an interesting use of this summative assessment.

Gifted or highly advanced students may best be tested using extended writing (essay) samples or projects mainly because it is much easier to make them higher level. For example, according to the New Bloom's Taxonomy, "creating" is the highest level of thinking, and the above questioning methods do not easily allow for that.

Teachers can find enrichment essay prompts and project ideas in their textbooks or online. For almost every unit of study, teachers might go to www.Google.com to find a wealth of assessment resources. Teachers should note that for gifted or highly advanced students, the more open ended the problem type the better some of them will respond. *The Democratic Differentiated Classroom* (Waterman, 2007), shows how I worked with gifted and highly advanced students using student-led unit planning. Many of the gifted students in my class worked amazingly hard on the projects they designed based on a theme the class chose. From that theme, they used a project to answer a specific essential question that they chose to address.

One of the most exciting processes related to assessment is the development of the "consensus rubric." Gifted or highly advanced students know how to set criteria and standards for their projects so that teachers can evaluate them based on the ideas they find important. Democratic differentiation is organic to differentiating instruction for gifted or highly advanced students; therefore, teachers may want to explore the model in more detail.

Extended Writing Assessments

One of the best ways to assess gifted or highly advanced students' learning is to assign an extended writing assessment.

Procedures

Figure 5.13 shows some suggested math and science topics for writing assignments categorized by "modes" of writing.

Figure 5.13. Math and Science Topics

Writing Mode	*Content*	*Prompt Ideas*
Descriptive	Math	♦ Choose a positive or negative number between 1 and 9. Make that number concrete in some way and describe it in rich detail. ♦ (For any graph or geometric figure created by a mathematical function or formula) Describe in vivid detail the picture created by the _____ (specific formula or function, such as a quadratic function) might make.
	Science	♦ Create a small planet and vividly describe what it looks like. Use these science terms in your description: landforms, atmosphere, habitat, topography, weather, life forms. ♦ (For any science content) Write a thorough and detailed description of _____ _____ (supply the topic, such as a plant cell).
Narrative	Math	♦ Create a word problem that includes the elements of a story, including the following: (1) a basic situation (exposition, which includes characters, setting, and what is going on), (2) a problem, which includes conflict and rising action (choosing the mathematical formula or strategy to solve it), (3) a climax (determining the solution), and (4) a resolution (which is the evaluation of the method and results of the manner in which the person solved the problem).
	Science	♦ Write a story that includes the science vocabulary and information from any science unit of study. For example, write a story about "how the chemical changed." Include the vocabulary terms listed at the beginning of the chapter (such as chemical property, endothermic and exothermic reaction) and information from this section of the book (or article) and make sure your story has interesting characters, setting, conflict, and resolution.

Writing Mode	Content	Prompt Ideas
Expository/ Informative	Math	♦ For any concept, write a detailed explanation of the mathematical processes involved. *Note: Show students how to organize their writing using the following:* 1. Organization–IBC form (introduction, body, conclusion) 2. Sufficient information using the following: (a) main ideas, (b) supporting details that provide examples, and (c) conclusions drawn from those ideas 3. Appropriate beginning and ending 4. Reasonable control of grammar, usage, and spelling *Note: Prompts could include asking students to show causes and effects or to write an extended definition.* Example prompt: Write a composition that thoroughly explains fractions.
	Science	♦ For any science topic, write a detailed explanation. *Note: use the information presented above as a general outline.* Example prompt: Write a composition explaining the effects of continental glaciers on global sea levels.
Persuasive/ Argumentative	Math	♦ For any math topic, write to argue a way of solving a specific problem. *Note: make sure there is more than one way to solve that problem. Students might verbalize their arguments prior to writing them or vice versa.* Example: What is the best way to find the percent of something?
	Science	♦ Numerous science topics lend themselves to persuasive prompts. *Note: encourage students to take a stand on an issue that affects their community and support their writing letters to the editor or to community leaders in an attempt to leverage real change.*

Twenty-First Century Projects

Gifted or highly advanced students are probably more connected to this century through technology skills than are many or most of their teachers. It is doing a disservice to these twenty-first century students if teachers do not allow them to (or show them how to) use the latest technological advances that might be useful as summative assessment vehicles.

Most teachers have some knowledge of allowing students to use PowerPoint presentations as a way to show what they have learned about a math or science topic; however, not as many teachers allow students to make other technology-based products such as films or podcasts. With any multimedia project for which students may gather pictures, music, or text from outside sources, comes the issue of copyright. Make sure that students understand copyright laws, especially the concept of "fair use." There are several sources for copyright policies. Teachers should choose the one or ones that they and their students will understand.

Film Making

Procedures

Step 1: Choose a topic or allow students to choose a topic based on interests and the material from the unit of study (including essential understandings and questions). Allow students to work alone, with a partner, or in a small (no more than four students) group.

Step 2: Provide students with a rubric template on which to develop criteria for a quality film.

Step 3: Group students according to the topics they have chosen. These groups view a student-made film that provides an excellent example and one that has problems. There are some excellent student film examples on www. myhero.com, www.studentfilms.com, or www.studentfilmmakers.com.

Step 4: The whole class discusses issues of quality and lack of quality. Following this discussion, students work together to create a rubric that reflects the discussion and their ideas.

Step 5: Collect these rubrics and consolidates them into one "class rubric."

Step 6: During the next class, share that rubric with the class and hand out the syllabus (see Figure 5.14 below).

Step 7: Provide each person, partnership, or group, a template and directions for how to construct a storyboard for a film. Two good resources for this information include http://www.storycenter.org/memvoice/pages/tutorial_3.html (which has a template and directions for completing a story board) or http://accad.osu.edu/womenandtech/storyboard%20.resource/. Google "storyboards" to find other resources if these are not adequate.

Step 8: Use a student-made short film and analyze it frame by frame to show students how the creator of the film might have used a story board. The class follows along recording the same information on their sheets of paper.

If there is time, show another very short film so that students might practice the process of making a storyboard on their own.

Step 9: With partners or in small groups, students create a rubric for evaluating their storyboards. As with the film rubric, make a composite rubric from among the student responses.

Step 10: Students may work either in class or at home to design their storyboards and then their films. Check on their progress periodically and encourage them to make an appointment with you or the media specialist to work on editing the film.

Step 11: You or the media specialist should help students edit their films using a film-editing program, and then students sign up to present.

Step 11: Students present and receive feedback from their peers and a grade from the teacher.

Figure 5.14. Filmmaking Syllabus

1. Choose a topic that addresses an important aspect of our unit of study.
   Date due: _____

2. Either work alone, find a partner, or work with a small group (no more than four). Submit your plan by: _____.

3. Create a storyboard for your film. Date due: _____.

4. Create your film. Date due: _____.

5. Make an appointment with the media specialist to get help editing your film.
   Date of appointment: _____.

6.   Sign up to present your film.

7.   Present the film on this date: _____

8.   Grade: _____

Comments:

Podcasting Procedures

Podcasting is a relatively new and exciting way for gifted or highly advanced students to show what they have learned from a unit of study. If teachers are interested in allowing their students to use a podcast as a summative assessment, they can familiarize themselves with this technology, or if they are not inclined to learn how to do it themselves, they might want to allow their tech-savvy students to use it. Podcasting involves creating a series of digital-media files that the student can distribute over the Internet using syndication feeds for playback on portable media players and computers. A podcast differs from other digital media formats because podcasters can syndicate their work, others can subscribe to it, and it is easy to download when the podcaster needs to add new content. The podcaster can add new content using an aggregator or feed reader capable of reading feed formats such as RSS or Atom.

What follows are the steps for teaching students to create a podcast. These steps were adapted from http://www.podcasingnews.come/article/How-to-podcas.html.

Step 1: Inform students that they will be creating a podcast. Ask students what they already know about podcasting to find out how to differentiate the instruction.

Step 2: Show at least one example of an excellent podcast and one of a not so excellent one, and as with the filmmaking unit, the students should create a rubric for evaluating both the podcast plan and the actual podcast.

Step 3: Students can work alone, with a partner, or in a small group to create the content for their show. Content could include interviews, music, commentary, or anything the students find interesting. Use a specific planning format or allow students to determine their own.

Step 4: After the student podcast plan has been assessed, help them record the audio using Audacity, an open source, cross-platform, and free resource that allow students to mix multiple audio files.

Step 5: Students should save their finished audio show at maximum quality in the native format of their audio application. Saving this allows students to edit or reuse their recording to have a good version.

Step 5: Once the students have their completed audio content, they need to convert their file to MP3 format. Using MP3 format allows universal access to the podcast. Students should use the minimum bit rate that provides good results. Here are some suggested settings:

- 48 to 56k mono—sermons, audio books, talk radio
- 64k+ stereo—music, music & talk combinations
- 128k stereo—good quality music

Students should make sure to save their work with a .mp3 file extension. (Students and teachers might read the article "Saving MP3 Files for Podcasting at this address: http://www.podcastingnews.com/article/saving-MP3-files-for-podcasting.html.)

Step 6: Students save their MP3 files on the webserver to test them with an MP3 player. The files can go anywhere on the site, but students may want to put all of them into one directory so they might be easy to find.

Step 7: Student next create a podcast newsfeed. These newsfeeds are RSS files that describe the podcast along with information for each show. An RSS file is a text tile that links students to their MP3 file. Student can read about RSS on http://www.podcastingnews.com/articles/Understanding_RSS_Feeds.html.

Step 8: Students can use any text editor to create an RSS news feed, however, most podcasters use blogging programs or other applications that automatically generate newsfeeds. If students use a blogging tool that lets them reference "enclosures," they should create an item for each MP3 file they publish, and they should use an URL of audio content as their enclosure. If the blogging tool does not support enclosures, students can edit their RSS file with any text editor to add the enclosure tag. An example can be found at the Trade Secrets podcast newsfeed: <enclosure url="http://static.podcatch.com/manila/gems/un/TS20041107.mp3" length="49885056" type="audio/mpeg"/>.

Students should understand that RSS newsfeeds normally show news items that contain a title, link, and description. Each item in a newsfeed provides meta-information about a URL on the web. For a podcast newsfeed, each item describes the content of an audio file that is referenced by the enclosure URL. Students should save their RSS file with a .rss or .xml extension. Students should have one newsfeed that holds all of their recent work from newest to oldest.

Step 9: Students should transfer their podcast RSS file to the webserver like they would save any other content. They should validate this using an online RSS validator. If the podcast newsfeed is valid, it is ready to be published to the World Wide Web. Students might develop a podcast logo and should publish their work on a podcast directory.

Step 10: Students should present their podcasts to the class to receive feedback from their peers and a grade from their teacher.

Other Useful Summative Assessments for Gifted or Highly Advanced Students

Gifted or highly advanced students thrive on novelty and chances to make choices about how they show what they know. The following is a short list of some of the best summative assessments for these students.

♦ *In-school field trip:* Allow students to develop classroom centers that address the content of a unit of study in math or science or math and science integrated topic. These centers could be a demonstration, a speaker, an exhibit, a game, a simulation, or an experiment. Students plan and develop these centers and offer them to the rest of the school as a field trip within the walls of the school. Teachers supply students with field-trip journals or assignment sheets in which they should record their learning and their reflections.

♦ *Book study:* The teacher identifies books that have science and/or math themes and asks students to read them to discover specific content. Students can write about these books, make an artistic project, or have a seminar discussion. The lives of great mathematicians and scientists are great ideas for this study. The whole class could read the book together, or students might select their own books to read. Some excellent books are: *Silent Spring* by Rachel Carson, *A Brief History of Time* by Stephen Hawking, *The Double Helix* by James D. Watson, and *The Hot Zone: A Terrifying True Story* by Richard Preston.

♦ *Trial simulation:* The teacher might think of a science or math topic that involves a crime. For example, the class could try a business that is polluting ground water and making a community sick or they could put the number zero on trial. The teacher can take the following steps to simulate a trial in the classroom.

Step 1: Ask students how they stand on the issue. The issue must have two distinct sides that students might take in a somewhat equal manner. Because this is a role-playing event, assign the following roles: three defense lawyers, three prosecution lawyers, a defendant, witnesses, and jury members. The teacher should be the judge.

Step 2: Present the role assignments as follows:

- Lawyers: Develop the case in writing including generating the questions they should ask the witnesses, their opening statement and their closing statement. They can develop props such as pretend X-rays and other supporting artifacts to support their cases.
- Witnesses: Write a brief description of their character and their stance on the issue; they role-play being questioned on the witness stand. Witnesses may use costumes and props (e.g., crutches and bandages).
- Jury: While the lawyers and witnesses are developing their piece of the process, the jury writes their stand on the issue. Someone can be the foreman.

Step 3: Set the class up as much like a courtroom as possible. The judge (teacher) begins the process. Ask the prosecution to make their opening statement (make a time limit, such as 5 minutes) and to question their witnesses. Next, allow the defense to make their case. After both have presented their cases, the prosecution makes a closing statement, and then the defense makes theirs. Finally the jury votes using a silent ballot to decide the fate of the defendant, and the foreman announces the results.

Summary

Gifted or highly advanced students can enjoy working with others or alone to solve open-ended problems and to respond to appropriate challenges. To differentiate assessment for them, teachers must understand them as a group and as individuals.

It may be challenging to construct assessments that motivate them and encourage them to do their best. The most successful assessments for these kinds of students ask students to think, evaluate, and create at high levels.

6

Putting It All Together

In this chapter teachers will see how to use the differentiating assessment six-part process with a composite secondary teacher's math unit differentiated by readiness using "tiering."

For this unit of study, teachers will see examples of how to apply the six-part process to implement differentiated assessment. What follows is a review of the overview of using six parts of planning differentiated assessment (Figure 6.1) and the Differentiating Assessment: Six-Part Template (Figure 6.2).

Figure 6.1. Six Parts of Planning Differentiated Assessment

1.	Students' Needs:	Who are the students in terms of: (a) readiness, (b) interests, and (c) learning and thinking styles, and what do they already know about the topic?
2.	Curriculum:	What enduring essential knowledge (EEK) (expressed as essential questions [EQ]) do these students need to know, understand, and do (KUD)? Note that the measurable objective(s) is listed separately in Part 3 but is also included in the curriculum.
3.	Measurable Objective:	How will teachers measure that learning?
4.	Differentiation:	How should teachers differentiate the assessment to meet their learning needs?
5.	Procedures:	What procedures will teachers follow to implement the assessment?
6.	Assessment Audit:	How will teachers evaluate the alignment of the assessment(s) and procedures so that they have a clear picture of what each student knows, understands, and can do related to the content?

Figure 6.2. Differentiating Assessment: Six-Part Template

1. Students' Needs (described in detail)				
2. Curriculum				
Standard course of study (SCOS)	Essential question (EQ)	Know	Understand	Do *(See MO below)*
3. Measurable Objectives **The generic template is as follows**				
Introduction	Thinking Verbs	Product	Response Criterion	Content
4. Differentiation				
Readiness		Interests		Learning Styles
5. Assessment Procedures (listed by steps)				
6. Assessment Audit				

Part 1: Students' Needs

Unless they have a special needs roster, most middle or high school teachers have between four and six classes of students for whom to plan units of study. They often have between 80 and 150 or more student contacts. These students will naturally have varied learning skills and deficiencies, interests, and styles of learning; therefore, to provide best assessments, teachers will need to plan all units of study using differentiated assessment. The usual secondary class roster will have some of the following general types of students:

- ♦ Learning disabled (LD) in reading, writing, math, or other—motivated or unmotivated.

- ♦ English language learner (ELL) for whom English is a second language—motivated or unmotivated

- ♦ At-risk learners several levels below grade—motivated or unmotivated

- ♦ Average ability- on grade level—motivated or unmotivated

♦ Gifted or highly advanced—motivated or unmotivated

♦ And many more types of students

The most challenging of the students are those who are unmotivated at any level. These students challenge teachers because of behavior issues and noncompliance with assignments. They cause class disruption and more work for teachers who have to constantly "ask" them to turn in their work. The examples that follow will show how teachers might plan unit assessments for classes that include all of the learning types previously mentioned (Figure 6.3). Therefore, Part 1 of the Differentiating Assessment: Six-Part Template will be the same for all three examples.

Math Unit Example

Figure 6.3. Math Unit on Using Bar and Line Graphs: Differentiated by Readiness Using Tiering

Students' Needs				
(See Part 1: Students' Needs for a description)				
Curriculum				
SCOS	**EQ:** How might students use line and bar graphs as presentations of data?	**K**now—How to solve problems with line and bar graphs, how to create a line and a bar graph, how to analyze and draw conclusions about line and bar graphs, the definitions of independent and dependent variables, collecting and charting data, choosing the best kind of graph to display data	**U**nderstand that line and bar graphs help us solve problems with and better understand important data about a variety of topics	**D**o—Define dependent and independent variables, collect and chart data, choose the best graph to display data, create a line and bar graph, analyze and draw conclusions about line and bar graphs *(See MO below)*

Measurable Objective 1				
Introduction	Thinking Verbs	Product	Response Criterion	Content
Students will…	recall, organize, classify, interpret, explain	to record data that represents independent and dependent variables	that are sufficient and accurate	on a variety of topics.

Measurable Objective 2				
Introduction	Thinking Verbs	Product (s)	Response Criterion	Content
Students will…	recall, organize, attribute, execute, classify, interpret, explain	to find solutions to problems presented by teacher and students	that are sufficient and accurate	using line and bar graphs.

Measurable Objective 3				
Introduction	Thinking Verb(s)	Product (s)	Response Criterion	Content
Students will…	generate, create, produce	♦ line graph ♦ bar graph	that are sufficient and accurate about	teacher and student-generated data.

Measurable Objective 4				
Introduction	Thinking Verb(s)	Product (s)	Response Criterion	Content
Students will…	analyze, attribute, differentiate, interpret	to answer questions and pose questions	that are sufficient and accurate for	teacher and student-generated data.

Differentiation		
Readiness—tiered lessons and assessments	**Interests**—students collect data for and analyze line and bar graphs	**Learning styles**—mastery, mathematical/logical, analytical

Procedures (Summarized)

1. Explain about and show students examples of how to create line and bar graphs. Use scaffolding (such as direct instruction and special teacher help, grouping, partnering, graphic organizers) to help students experience creating bar and line graphs.

2. Assess students' ability to create line and bar graphs with engaging data that teachers or students supply.

3. Explain how to analyze and draw conclusions from information presented in line and bar graphs.

4. Assess students' ability to analyze and draw conclusions from increasingly difficult line and bar graphs.

Procedures (Expanded)

Day 1: *Conduct a preassessment.* This aspect of assessment also fits into Part 1 of the differentiated assessment process.

Preassessment

For this unit of study, teachers may want to know from each student what he or she can do in terms of using line and bar graphs to display data. For this reason, teachers might use a pretest from their textbook, or they might write five typical problems that will help determine if students understand how to display data on bar or line graphs.

Figure 6.4 is a five-question quiz to determine students' abilities to display data on a bar or line graph.

Figure 6.4. Quiz: What Do You Know about Bar and Line Graphs?

1. Make a line graph using these data points:

   $x = 2, y = 2$

   $x = 4, y = 5$

   $x = 6, y = 8$

   $x = 8, y = 9$

2. Make a bar graph using this information:

   In our class, 2 students made an A, 5 students made a B, 10 students made C, 3 students made a D, and 4 students made an F.

3. Think of an example of data that you might best display on a line or bar graph. Why did you choose that kind of graph?

4. For question 2, which variables are dependent, and which are independent?

5. Interpret the following graphs.

Bar Graph Quiz

Actions	Number
Visiting friends	14
Talking to friends on the telephone	13
Playing a sport	10
Working to make money	8
Using a computer	5

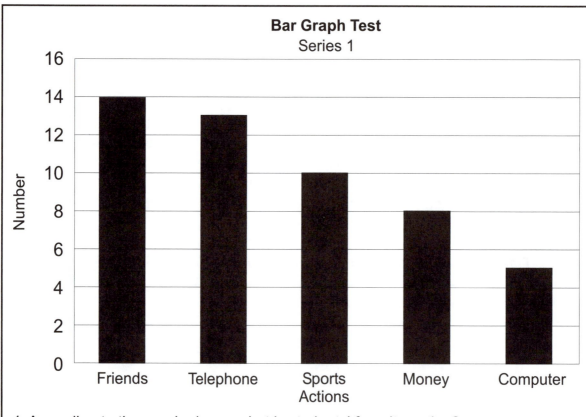

Bar Graph Test
Series 1

1. According to the graph above, what is students' favorite action?

    A.   Being with friends

    B.   Using the telephone

    C.   Earning money

    D.   Using a computer

2. According to the graph above, what is students' least favorite action?

   A.   Being with friends

   B.   Using the telephone

   C.   Earning money

   D.   Using a computer

3. According to the graph above, which two actions have the most similar number of interested students?

   A.   Being with friends and using a computer

   B.   Play sports and earning money

   C.   Talking on the telephone and visiting with friends

   D.   Talking on the telephone and playing a sport

   E. Using the telephone

   F. Earning money

   G. Using a computer

4. How many students most enjoyed using a computer?

   A. 14

   B. 10

   C. 8

   D. 5

5. True or false: Based on this bar graph would you say more students liked being with others or being alone?

   A. True

   B. False

Adapted from http://www.mcwdn.org/Graphs/BarGraph.html, accessed July 8, 2008.

I created the above bar graph by using an Excel program that allowed me to plug in data and then to create a graph. Teachers may want to teach students this technology skill if they don't already have it. Also, teachers can go online to http://www.super teacherworksheets.com/graphing.html to find free worksheets of bar graph assessments easy, medium, and difficult.

Teachers might have students read from a math textbook, view a PowerPoint presentation, and work some line and bar graph problems. They can choose to use some of these informal assessments as they are presenting information about graphs. Information will include practicing determining independent and dependent variables, plugging in data points, and so forth.

Informal Assessments

Use the following informal assessments for these specific reasons.

♦ Seven Hands Raised is used to determine if students understand content.

♦ Kinesthetic or floor math help teachers assess students' understanding of line and bar graphs by having them demonstrate representing data by lining up in bars. For example, all the students with a certain color shirt, or hair, or other, could line up together as a bar. Or, teachers could give students yarn and ask them to make a line graph using the floor tiles as graph paper.

♦ 3-2-1 (the ticket out the door) could be three new ideas, two ways to use graphs, and one question.

♦ Leveled homework: By now the teacher and students will have some idea of how well students understand this content. For our purposes, we will say that the teacher determined from the preassessment that there are approximately three distinct levels of student readiness to learn about bar and line graphs. The teacher might suggest a level to each student or allow each student to choose one of the three levels of homework with which he or she feels most comfortable (Figure 6.5).

Figure 6.5. Leveled Homework

Level 1	Level 2	Level 3
Students will collect and chart the following data (see graphic support below): Find out when 15 students have birthdays. Categorize their birthdays by seasons (fall, winter, spring, and fall) and put the correct numbers in the chart provided.	Students will collect data on the amount of time they spend doing various activities during the day. For example: time spent in school, time spent riding the bus, etc. Students will choose the categories and complete the partial chart below.	Students choose a dependent and independent variable on which to collect data. Students create a chart for the data. (These students should be able to create their own chart including categories and dependent and independent variables.)

Level 1: Data Chart

Birthdays by Seasons	Number of Students
Fall (September 22–December 21)	
Winter (December 22–March 21)	
Spring (March 22–June 21)	
Summer (June 22–September 21)	

Level 2: Data Chart

Activities	Time Spent
Attending school	
Riding the bus home	

Students complete the chart on their own.

Level 3: On Their Own

Day 2: Group students by the homework they completed and allow them to share their products with members of their group. Be available for questions and other kinds of assistance. Take an informal assessment of students' abilities based on this homework. Regroup students as follows:

Group 1: Students who did not complete or master their homework

Group 2: Students who did well on Level 1

Group 3: Students who did well on Level 2

Group 4: Students who did well on Level 3

Next, explain how students might use Excel to make charts from data. If you do not have access to Excel, students will practice making graphs from the data they collected for their homework. Students who have no data will use data supplied by the teacher. Assess students' ability to make a bar graph and a line graph from their data. Their graphs will be their ticket out the door. Students will choose from among three levels of homework as shown in Figure 6.6.

Figure 6.6. Leveled Homework

Level 1	Level 2	Level 3
Do Level 2 homework from last class.	Do Level 3 homework from last class.	Find a line or bar graph from an online or hard copy source. Write three questions about the line or bar graph.

Day 3 and so on: Determine at this point, based on students' mastery of homework, if they are "ready" to deal with increasingly difficult processes of problem solving using line and/or bar graphs. Use problems from the textbook or use various websites that have line and bar graph problems. *Math: Bar, Line, and Picture Graphs* (http://www.emints.org/ethemes/resources/S00000791.shtml) is an online source of line and bar graph problems from eThemes that includes examples of several types of graphs and provides at least 14 links to interactive and demonstration websites. This site is an exceptional extension of teacher textbook resources.

To level study of bar and line graphs, teachers will pose increasingly difficult questions that require students to create, analyze, and draw conclusions about line and bar graphs. Teachers should flexibly group students so that at all times they are working in their zone of proximal development. This means that they can work independently with some coaching from teachers or fellow students. Teachers will constantly collect assigned work, offer constructive feedback, and flexibly group students until they are ready to conduct a summative assessment.

Summative Assessment Choices

Teachers might use a standardized measure of student achievement that matches state or district standards. Teachers might level the assessment as a means of vertically articulating curriculum standards for future grade-level requirements. For example, if students need higher skill levels for advanced classes, teachers might inspire students at any mastery level to exceed grade-level standards.

Summary

In this chapter, I have shown how to use various types of assessments together to teach a unit of study. Unless they have a highly specialized roster, most secondary teachers face a wide variety of student needs. It is critical that teachers learn as much as they can about how to meet their students where they are to facilitate their movement toward learning.

References

Allen, R. (2007) *TrainSmart: Effective training every time.* Thousand Oaks, CA: Corwin Press.

Aronson, E., Blaney, N., Stephan, C., Sikes, J., & Snapp, M. (1978). *The jigsaw classroom.* Beverly Hills, CA: Sage Publication.

Alderman, M. (1990). Motivation for at-risk students. *Educational Leadership, 48,* 27–30.

Anderson, L., Krathwohl, D., Airasian, P., Cruikshank, K., Mayer, R., Pintrich, P., et al. (Eds.) (2001). *A taxonomy for learning, teaching, and assessing: a revision of Bloom's taxonomy of educational objectives.* New York: Longman.

Ausubel, D. (1963). *The psychology of meaningful verbal learning,* New York: Grune & Stratton.

Ausubel, D. (1968). *Educational psychology, a cognitive view.* New York: Holt, Rinehart, & Winston.

Belvel, P., & Jordan, M. (2003). *Rethinking classroom management: Strategies for prevention, intervention, and problem solving.* Thousand Oaks, CA: Corwin Press, Inc.

Bruner, J. (1973). *Beyond the information given: Studies in the psychology of learning.* Oxford: W. W. Norton.

Butler, K. (1984). *Learning and teaching styles in theory and practice.* Columbia, CT: Learner's Dimension.

Butler, K. (1987). Successful learning strategies for the emerging adolescent. *Oklahoma middle level education association journal,* 1–7.

DeVries, D., Edwards, K., & Slavin, R. (1978). Biracial learning teams and race relations in the classroom: Four field experiments using teams-games-tournaments. *Journal of Educational Psychology, 70(3),* 356–362.

Dunn, R., & Dunn, K. (1993). *Teaching secondary students through their individual learning styles: practical approaches for grades 7–12.* Boston, MA: Allyn and Bacon.

Erikson, E. (1950). *Childhood and society.* New York: Norton.

Fisher, D., & Frey, N. (2007) *Checking for understanding: formative assessment techniques for your classroom.* Alexandria, VA: Association for Supervision and Curriculum Development.

Fulwiler, T. (1980). Journals across the disciplines. *English Journal, 69(9),* 14–19.

Gardner, H. (1993). *Multiple intelligences: the theory and practice.* New York: Basic Books.

Gick, M., & Holyoak, K. (1980). Analogical problem solving. *Cognitive Psychology, 12,* 306–355.

Ginn, W. (2003). *Jean Piaget—intellectual development.* Accessed September 20, 2003, at http://www.sk.com.br/sk-paige.htm.

Gordon, W. (1961). *Synectices: The development of creative capacity.* New York: Harper.

Herber, H. (1978). *Teaching reading in the content areas.* Englewood Cliffs, NJ: Prentice Hall.

Hunter, R. (2004). *Madeline Hunter's mastery teaching: Increasing instructional effectiveness in elementary and secondary schools.* (Updated edition.) Thousand Oaks, CA: Corwin Press.

Jones, V., & Jones, L. (1990). *Comprehensive classroom management: Motivating and managing students* (3rd Ed.). Boston, MA: Allyn and Bacon.

Kagan, S. (1997). *Cooperative learning.* San Clemente, CA: Kagan Professional Development.

Keene, E., & Zimmerman, S. (1997). *Mosaic of thought: teaching comprehension in a reader's workshop.* Portsmouth, NH: Heinemann.

Marzano, R. (2003). *What works in schools.* Alexandria, VA: Association for Supervision and Curriculum Development.

Marzano, R., Pickering, D., & Pollock, J. (2001). *Classroom instruction that works: Research-based strategies for increasing student achievement.* Alexandria, VA: Association for Supervision and Curriculum Development.

McCarthy, B. (1981). *The 4-mat system: Teaching to learning styles with right/left mode techniques.* Wauconda, IL: About Learning.

Mosston, M. (1972). *Teaching: From command to discovery.* Belmont, CA: Wadsworth Publishing.

Northey, S. (2005). *Handbook on differentiating instruction in middle and high school.* Larchmont, NY: Eye on Education.

O'Brien, L. (1990). *Learning channels; Preference checklist.* Philadelphia, PA; Research for Better Schools.

Ogle, D. (1986). A teaching model that develops active reading of expository text. *The Reading Teacher, 39*(6), 564–570.

Opitz, M., & Rasinski, T. (1998). *Good-bye round robin: 25 effective oral reading strategies.* Portsmouth, NH: Heinemann.

Rief, L. (1998). *Vision and voice: Expanding the literacy spectrum.* Portsmouth, NH: Heinemann.

Sagor, R., & Cox, J. (2004). *At-risk students: Reaching and teaching them* (2nd Ed.). Larchmont, NY: Eye On Education.

Santa, C., & Havens, I. (1991). Learning through writing. In C. Santa & D. Alvermann (Eds.), *Science learning: processes and applications*. Newark, DE: International Reading Association.

Schoenbach, R., Greenleaf, C., Cziko, C., & Hurwitz, L. (1999). *Reading for understanding: a guide to improving reading in middle and high school classrooms: the reading apprenticeship guidebook*. San Francisco: Jossey-Bass.

Silver, H., Strong, W., & Perini, M. (2007). *The strategic teacher: selecting the right research-based strategy for every lesson*. Alexandria, VA: Association for Supervision and Curriculum Development.

Silver, H., & Strong, R. (2004) *Learning Style Inventory for Students*. Ho-Ho-Kus, NJ: Thoughtful Education Press.

Silver, H., Strong, R., & Perini, M. (2001). *Teaching what matters most: Standards and strategies for raising student achievement*. Alexandria, VA: Association for Supervision and Curriculum Development.

Sternberg, R. (1997). *Thinking styles*. New York, NY: Cambridge University Press.

Stiggins, R., Arter, J., Chappuis, J., & Chappuis, S. (2006). *Classroom assessment for student learning: doing it right-using it well*. Upper Saddle River, NJ; Merrill/Prentice Hall.

Strong, R., Silver, H., Perini, & Tuculescu, G. (2002). *Reading for academic success: Powerful strategies for struggling average and advanced readers, grades 7–12*. Thousand Oaks, CA: Corwin Press.

Strong, R., Hanson, J., & Silver, H. (1995). *Questioning styles and strategies* (3rd ed.) Woodbridge, NJ: Thoughtful Education Press.

Suchman, J. (1966). *Developing inquiry*. Chicago, IL: Science Research Associates.

Taba, H. (1971). *Hilda Taba teaching strategies program*. Miami, FL: Institute for Staff Development.

Taba, H. (1962). *Curriculum development, theory and practice*. New York: Harcourt Brace & World.

Tomlinson, C. (1995). *How to differentiate instruction in mixed-ability classrooms*. Alexandria, VA: Association for Supervision and Curriculum Development.

Tomlinson, C. (1999). *The differentiated classroom: responding to the needs of all learners*. Alexandria, VA: Association for Supervision and Curriculum Development.

Tomlinson, C. (2003). *Differentiation in practice: a resource guide for differentiating curriculum, grades 5–9*. Alexandria, VA: Association for Supervision and Curriculum Development.

Tovani, C. (2000). *I read it, but I don't get it: comprehension strategies for adolescent readers*. Portland, Me: Stenhouse.

Trussell-Cullen, A. (1998). *Assessment: in the learner-centered classroom*. Carlsbad, CA: Dominie Press.

Vygotsky, L. (1978). Interaction between learning and development. In M. Cole, V. John-Steiner, S. Scribner, & E. Souberman, (Eds.), *Mind in society: The development of higher psychological process.* (pp. 79-92). Cambridge, MA: Harvard University Press.

Waterman, S. (2007). *The democratic differentiated classroom.* Larchmont, NY: Eye On Education.

Weiner, B. (1985). An attributional theory of motivation and emotion. *Psychological Review, 92,* 548–573.

Wiggins, G., & McTighe, J. (1998). *Understanding by design.* Alexandria, VA: Association for Supervision and Curriculum Development.

Wormeli, R. (2006). *Fair isn't always equal: assessing and grading in the differentiated classroom.* Portland, ME: Stenhouse.

Wood, K. (2001). *Strategies for integrating reading and writing.* Winterville, OH: National Middle School Association.

Wu, B. (1999). *The Internet, computer games, and morality: ethics, technology, and science.* Accessed from ThinkQuest.org. April 18, 2008, at http://www.thinkquest.org/29435.main.html.